Goal Analysis

ROBERT F. MAGER

fp FEARON PUBLISHERS

Lear Siegler, Inc., Education Division • Belmont, California

Books by Robert F. Mager

Goal Analysis
Analyzing Performance Problems
    (with Peter Pipe)
Developing Attitude Toward Learning
Developing Vocational Instruction
    (with Kenneth M. Beach, Jr.)
Preparing Instructional Objectives

371.102
M 272

Library of Congress Catalog Card Number: 77–189630

Printed in the United States of America.

FOR

Walt Thorne,	whose mind I can lean on;
Margo Hicks,	whose help I can count on;
John Warriner,	whose infinitives I can split on;
Jack Vaughn,	who always knows one when he sees one;
Sturmun Drang,	who never knows one when he sees one; and
Harnicky Hirsute,	who has never been seen at all.

Preface

Once upon a time in the land of Fuzz, King Aling called in his cousin Ding and commanded, "Go ye out into all of Fuzzland and find me the goodest of men, whom I shall reward for his goodness."

"But how will I know one when I see one?" asked the Fuzzy.

"Why, he will be *sincere*," scoffed the king, and whacked off a leg for his impertinence.

So, the Fuzzy limped out to find a good man. But soon he returned, confused and empty-handed.

"But how will I know one when I see one?" he asked again.

"Why, he will be *dedicated*," grumbled the king, and whacked off another leg for his impertinence.

So the Fuzzy hobbled away once more to look for the goodest of men. But again he returned, confused and empty-handed.

"But how will I know one when I see one?" he pleaded.

"Why, he will have *internalized his growing awareness*," fumed the king, and whacked off another leg for his impertinence.

So the Fuzzy, now on his last leg, hopped out to continue his search. In time, he returned with the wisest, most sincere and dedicated Fuzzy in all of Fuzzland, and stood him before the king.

"Why, this man won't do at all," roared the king. "He is much too thin to suit me." Whereupon, he whacked off the last leg of the Fuzzy, who fell to the floor with a squishy thump.

The moral of this fable is that . . . *if you can't tell one when you see one, you may wind up without a leg to stand on.*

IF YOU CAN'T TELL ONE WHEN YOU SEE ONE, YOU MAY WIND UP WITHOUT A LEG TO STAND ON.

If your goals are important to achieve, it is essential that you do more than just talk about them in "Fuzzy" terminology. Broad statements of intent can be achieved only to the degree that their meaning is understood, *to the degree that you will know one when you see one.*

And that is what *Goal Analysis* is about. Goal analysis is a procedure useful in helping you describe the *meaning* of the goals you hope to achieve, whether these goals deal with attitudes, appreciations, or understandings. It is *not* the object of this book to tell you what to achieve or what you should mean by the words you use. The sole purpose is to help you understand your own intents better so that you will be able to make better decisions toward their achievement and be able to recognize progress and success.

If you have ever asked questions like these:

What do you do about the affective domain?
Why don't they have the right attitude?
How can I help them understand?
How can I motivate them?
How can I deepen their appreciation?

Goal Analysis will help you find the answers.

R. F. MAGER

Contents

PART I

Why To Do It

What It's All About

There never seems to be a shortage of "teaching." Thousands of courses are offered by thousands of institutions — public, private, industrial, vocational, and academic. Parents begin instructing their offspring almost as soon as the umbilical cord is tied. (For years after, they can be seen waving their fingers and intoning such profundities as "I'll . . . teach . . . *you!*") Then the schools take over, followed by the military, the employer, the college, and almost anyone else who has the urge. Now there is even talk of "lifelong learning," as if that were not already the case.

Why in the world?

Why must a person spend a significant part of his life trying to be *different* than he is? Are we so universally incompetent that we cannot be left alone to grow and mature for even a minute without someone constantly "teaching at" us? Why is it that there are so many people from so many walks of life engaged in the pursuit called "instruction"?

3

It must be that a lot of people want to be different from what they are, or that a lot of people think a lot of *other* people ought to be different from what they are; for the only legitimate justification for instruction is the reduction or elimination of a genuine difference between what someone *can* do and what he or someone else would *like* him to be able to do. If there is *no* difference between actual and desired capability, if a person is already in the condition he wants to be in or is expected to be in, instruction is not only unjustified, it may even be considered fraudulent.

If there *is* a genuine difference between what a person can do or what he or someone else wants him to be able to do, it may be that instruction will help. But only maybe. To underscore the point, consider this nutty dialogue between a doctor (hypothetical) and a woman.

Doc: Ah, good morning, madam.

Mad: Good morning, doctor.

Doc: Just a moment and I'll have your prescription all written out.

Mad: Wait a minute . . .

Doc: No time like the present, you know.

Mad: But I haven't even told you why I'm here yet.

Doc: No need. I've been a doctor for seventeen years.

Mad: Don't you even *examine* people?

Doc: What for? I've been trained by one of the best schools, and I *know* what most people need in the way of treatment.

Mad: You give everybody the same treatment?

Doc: Of course. Saves time.

Mad: That's crazy!

Doc: Not at all. Most patients improve. Some improve more than others, of course, but that's mostly because they try harder.

Mad: What about the ones who get worse?

Doc: No problem. I label them as failures and send them on . . . and on . . . and on. Ah, by the way, why *are* you here?

Mad: I *was* the new cleaning lady. And good-by!

Like medication, instruction can be given when none is needed. It is also possible, as in prescribing medication, to instruct when some *other* remedy would be more to the point. Therefore, it is as appropriate for those who would solve problems of human performance to perform an analysis before selecting a remedy as it is for a physician to make a diagnosis before prescribing a cure.

Put another way, if teaching is going to be successful, there must be a connection between the problem and the solution, between the *need* for instruction and the *nature* of the instruction. Wherever instruction exists, one should be able to see the connection between that instruction and the reason for its existence.

Since there are many instances in which instruction is the proper solution, the connection can be seen quite readily. A person who is learning to weld is receiving relevant instruction . . . if he wants to be a welder. Instruction in club-swinging will help solve the problem . . . of those who want to be golfers. If an oboe player is turned down by an orchestra because he doesn't know the score, instruction in score-reading should help solve *his* problem.

Often, however, the connection between the outcome desired and what must be done to achieve it is not so apparent. To caricature the point, consider this goofy dialogue between a student and a college professor (hypothetical, of course).

Stud: I refuse to pay you for this course.

Prof: Why? Didn't I teach you how to make the finest buggy whips ever created?

Stud: Yes, you did.

Prof: Well then?

Stud: But I took this course because I wanted to understand history.

Prof: Can you deny that buggy whips were used by some
of the most important men in history?

Stud: I suppose not.

Prof: Can you deny that buggy whips are an integral part
of history?

Stud: I don't know. I never learned any history. I only
learned how to make buggy whips.

Prof: But wasn't I successful in teaching you how to make
good buggy whips?

Stud: Yes. But the fact remains . . .

Prof: Yes?

Stud: You didn't solve my problem.

It seems pretty obvious that if your goal is to improve
someone's understanding of history, you don't proceed to
make him an expert buggy whip maker. Nor would you
instruct him in welding or weaving. But what *would* you
teach him? What skills or knowledge are relevant to increasing his "understanding"? What does understanding
mean?

To take other examples, what should be the object of
instruction if the goal is to make "better citizens"? What
are the objectives of instruction if the goal is to achieve
"good judgment," "perceptive listening," "motivated workers," or "effective therapists"? Though these states may be
among the most important to achieve—and all goals *sound*
important—*the act of stating them does little to suggest the means
of their achievement.*

Actually, there are a number of procedures available that
will not only help determine *whether* instruction is a relevant
remedy for a problem of human performance, but also help

suggest what instruction is likely to be *appropriate* to the problem. To help show just where goal analysis fits into the larger scheme of things, a brief description of each of the five major procedures follows.

Performance Analysis.   A performance analysis is used to determine whether there is an important difference between what someone is *already* able to do and what it is *intended* for him to be able to do, and, if an important difference does exist, whether instruction or some other course of action (inform, manage, ignore) is appropriate. For example, if an instructor should conclude that his students aren't "properly motivated," a performance analysis would reveal the differences between the actual performances of the students and those desired by the instructor. If analysis shows that the students already know how to perform as expected but for some reason don't do so, the analysis would suggest the kind of action that would be useful in decreasing the difference between what *is* and what is *wanted*. In this example, that action is not likely to take the form of more instruction.

Task Analysis.   A task analysis is a careful description of what the competent person does or is supposed to do when he is doing a job. From this description, it is possible to derive *outcomes* for instruction that are tied closely to the *reason* for instruction. If, for example, the intent is to enable someone to perform as a brain surgeon, the task analysis would require the *observation* of competent surgeons in action and the detailed description of each observed and implied step in their performance. Once we know what the competent brain surgeon *does* when he's surging, it is possible to select instructional outcomes (objectives) that will more likely fulfill the reason for the instruction — developing another brain surgeon.

Critical Incident Analysis. A critical incident analysis (sometimes called a significant incident analysis) describes the indications that things are *not* going as desired. It answers the questions, What isn't happening *right*? or What isn't happening right *enough*? If the things that aren't going as expected lead to some important consequences, there are likely to be some strong clues about what should be done. If one of those things is instruction, that instruction will be tied closely to what the competent person is expected to do.

For example, the head of a nursing faculty recently decided to lengthen the in-service training by a four-hour block of instruction. To help decide what to teach, she sent a questionnaire to her faculty asking for suggestions. Had she carried out a critical incident analysis first and, for example, asked the hospital records what wasn't going as well as expected, she would have found some important clues. For one thing, she may have found a 5 to 15 percent medication error; that is, instances in which patients were given the wrong medication, somebody else's medication, or no medication at all. Since the consequence of medication error can be potentially bothersome, this would have been a clear call for some kind of action; here is a reason to "do" something. If, upon analysis, it becomes clear that instruction is a relevant part of the "doing," then objectives for that instruction intended to reduce the size of the problem can be derived from the critical incidents.

Target Population Description. A target population description is a careful examination of the characteristics (ability, education, interests, etc.) of those for whom instruction is intended. In this case, the information goes more toward *adjustment* of intended outcomes than their initial selection. Suppose, for example, one were to organize instruction aimed at teaching people to use a slide rule. What would be the objectives of that instruction? First, you would take a good *look* (task analysis) at some people who do a competent job of operating a slide rule and derive some objectives from that information. Next, you would find out what the common errors are in the use of the slide rule, as made by beginners and also by those more competent (critical incident analysis), and add to or subtract from your earlier objectives the objectives indicated by the results. Then, you would review in detail the characteristics of those intended to learn the skill and match their *existing* skills against the *desired* skills. If, for example, the prospective slide-rule drivers didn't know how to place decimal points, it wouldn't make much sense to design instruction that *assumed* they had this skill. In such cases, some adjustment must be made. One either specifies these skills as prerequisites to the instruction, or one decides to include those skills in the instruction. In either case, detailed knowledge of the target population assists in the derivation of meaningful instructional outcomes.

Goal Analysis. A person is often expected to perform in ways that are not reflected in tasks or errors. In addition to performing certain skills, he is supposed to "develop proper customer attitude" or "take pride in his work." Since it isn't possible to watch him developing or internalizing, and if these are important states to achieve, how will you proceed? How will you decide *if* instruction will help achieve the desired state; and, if it will, how will you decide *what kind* of instruction to organize?

A task analysis won't help, because there is no task to observe. A critical incident analysis won't help, because there are no errors or problems to tabulate. A target population description is useful mainly as an adjustment procedure on existing instructional objectives, so that is out. Likewise, a performance analysis can't be carried out until the relevant performances are identified.

This is where goal analysis fits. The function of goal analysis is to define the indefinable, to tangibilitate the intangible — to help us say what we mean by our important but abstract goals (or *fuzzies*, as they will be called in this book). With this procedure, it is possible to describe the essential elements of abstract states — to identify the main performances that go to make up the meaning of the goal. Once we know the performances that collectively define the goal, we will be in a better position to decide which of these performances need to be taught and which to be managed. Then we can select the most appropriate teaching or management procedures and arrange to measure our progress toward success.

Procedures To Follow To Help You . . .	Define Success So You Can . . .	Select the Strategy for Achieving It
Performance Analysis		Inform
Task Analysis	Desired Performances (Outcomes)	Instruct
Critical Incident Analysis		Manage
Target Population Description		Ignore
Goal Analysis		

Goals come in all sorts of shapes and sizes and are wrapped in all sorts of words. Some are stated briefly; others are not. One thing they have in common is that they all sound important. Sample the following:

be a good citizen
appreciate music
have a favorable attitude toward justice
understand man's disturbance of his environment
be a well-informed consumer
appreciate the problems of the twentieth-century world

By "important" is meant that there is some urgency to achieving certain desired outcomes, that undesirable consequences are likely to follow if certain outcomes are *not* achieved. Either a desirable outcome will fail to occur or an undesirable outcome will be likely to occur if the goal is not achieved or achieved more effectively than is now the case. Goals of importance deserve more effort toward their achievement than mere assertion of their importance. And again, that's where goal analysis comes in.*

THE GOAL OF THIS BOOK

The goal of this book is to help you "know when and how to do a goal analysis." But that's a fuzzy. It sounds nice, but it doesn't tell you *how to know one when you see one.* It points in the direction of the desired outcomes, but it doesn't describe them very well.

Aha! This is just the situation that calls for a goal analysis. Having performed one on this very fuzzy, I can now be more specific in telling you what it means.

The goal "know when and how to do a goal analysis" means:

1. Be able to identify statements that describe abstractions and those that describe performances.
2. Having identified a goal that you consider important to achieve, be able to describe the performances that represent your meaning of the goal. In other words, be able to describe specific outcomes that, if achieved, will cause you to agree that the goal is also achieved.

As a test of your success with the procedure, you would select a goal you think important, carry out the procedure, and then answer the question, If a person exhibited the performances I have described in a way I have described, would

---

*In scientific circles, this procedure is called "developing an operational definition." No matter. It doesn't do much good to have the name and not the skill.

I agree that he has achieved (represents) my goal? When you are able to answer yes, you will be finished with the analysis. If your answer is no, further analysis would be indicated.

If you are to analyze abstractions, you need to be sure you know one when you see one; so that will be considered next. But first (no, not a commercial) you have a choice:

If you are comfortable with the knowledge that statements about attitudes and appreciations are statements about abstractions, you might well skip the next chapter and go directly to Chapter 3.

If, on the other hand, you feel a little shaky about the idea that statements about attitudes and appreciations are statements about abstractions and are always inferred from circumstantial evidence, you might run through Chapter 2 on your way to Chapter 3.

Where's Your Attitude?

What does your doctor do when you ask him, Am I healthy? How does he determine your state of health? What does it take to cause him to use that abstract term in relation to your condition? He looks at specifics. He takes your blood pressure, counts your pulse — checks your reflexes and kicks your tires. He looks for a great number of specific indicators that, taken collectively, are the basis for statements about health. If most of these indicators are positive (no sign of trouble), he is willing to say you are healthy. The point is, when you want to find out if you are healthy, a doctor doesn't check your health; he checks specific physiological indicators and uses them as his basis for judgments about health. The specifics collectively define the abstract.

Now let's consider abstractions in general — and attitudes in particular. The main reason we don't succeed too well with attitudes is that we just don't know what we are talking about when we use the term. One hears teachers saying things like, "Today I'm teaching a cognitive lesson; tomorrow I'm going

to do an affective one,"* as though they believed they had
some control over *whether* they influenced someone's attitude, as though they didn't know that they influence attitude
whether they like it or not. One also hears comments such as,
"We've got to *teach* them to have the right attitude," implying that attitudes are mainly influenced by cognitive les-
sons, by teaching someone to know something he didn't
know before. It is as though they have forgotten that the
cognitive and psychomotor have to do with what a person
can do, and the affective with what he *will do*.

But think about it for a moment. Just what *do* we mean
when we use the word "attitude"? Is attitude a thing?

Well, no. Not a thing like a meringue or a mukluk. *Things*
are what you can poke with your fingers or beat with a stick.
Attitudes are not that sort of thing. You can't dissect someone and take out his attitude any more than you can dissect
him and take out his laugh. That doesn't mean that attitudes
and laughter don't exist; it's just that they aren't directly
available for physical examination — or for poking or pinching.

*If words like "cognitive" and "affective" disturb you, do what I do. When you
see *cognitive*, think "knowing"; when you see *affective*, think "feeling"; and when you
see *psychomotor*, think "doing." This oversimplifies things, it is true; but at least you
don't lose out when someone uses special words when ordinary ones will do.

So if attitude isn't a thing, what is it?

Attitude is a word, that's what it is. And words mean whatever their users want them to mean. (This one seems to have more misusers than users.)

By attitude, we generally mean to describe an abstraction, some sort of general state or condition existing inside ourselves or others. When someone says, "He has a favorable attitude toward mukluks," he is suggesting that the person will behave in one way when faced with a mukluk rather than in another. He is suggesting that the mukluk-lover will tend to say favorable things about the object, that he will tend to move toward the object when he sees one rather than away from it, and that he will tend to seek out ways to come into contact with the object. Similarly, a person who is said to have a favorable attitude toward music would be expected to say favorable things about the activity, to respond favorably when in the presence of the activity, and to seek out ways of increasing the amount of time that he *is* in the presence of the activity.

An interesting thing about attitudes is that every statement about attitude is a statement of prediction. No matter what someone says about the attitude of someone else, he is making a prediction about how that person is likely to behave in the future. Based on what he has seen someone do or heard him say in the past, he predicts how he will perform in the future. If you see me turn a bowl of fish soup over the cook's head, you might be urged to comment: "He has a negative attitude toward fish soup." Such a comment is based on what you saw me do, and is intended to predict that putting me in the presence of fish soup will be followed by some sort of negative act or comment on my part (toward the soup). You might be right or wrong, but the statement about attitude is a statement of prediction, a statement that intends to suggest how I might behave in some future time.

Since an attitude is not directly visible, it follows that all statements about attitude are based on circumstantial evidence that takes the form of visible behavior. If you hadn't seen me dump the fish soup on the cook, or heard or read an account of the fish story, you would have had no basis whatever for making a statement about how I am likely to behave in the presence of fish soup. You might be *wrong* in your attitude statement (your prediction); it might be the cook I dislike and not the fish soup. No problem; lots of people make incorrect predictions from the information available to them. The point is simply that, right or wrong, *a statement about attitude is a statement of prediction based on what somebody says or what somebody does.*

The behaviors on which attitude statements are made can properly be called *indicator behaviors*, for they are used as indicators of attitude. Indicators are a common item of our existence. We use thermometers to indicate temperature, speedometers to indicate speed, and voltmeters to indicate voltage. In each case, we use some sort of device to tell us the state or condition of something we cannot see or measure directly.

Some indicators are better than others. A voltmeter is a better indicator of the amount of voltage present in a circuit than the sensation you feel when you grab the wire. The loudness of the "ouch" is not directly related to the amount of the voltage; if you hired a wire-grabbing Ouchman and tried to measure the amount of voltage from the loudness of his ouches, you would have less success than if you employed a voltmeter.

The same holds true for attitudes and their indicator behaviors. Some behaviors are better indicators (predictors) of attitude than others, and it isn't always easy to tell which is better. To make it more difficult, any particular behavior might well be an indicator of any number of attitudes. When

I poured the fish soup on the cook, he couldn't tell whether that behavior was indicating a distaste for fish soup, *his* version of fish soup, fat cooks, fur-lined soup bowls, or dirty aprons. In the absence of some other indicators (behaviors) on my part, he could predict pretty well *that* I found something distinctly not to my liking, but not *what*. He would need more behavior on my part if he wanted to be sure. If, while carrying out the deed, I spoke thusly: "Sir, my distaste for fish soup is exceeded only by my distaste for fish stew," he would have a better clue as to how to interpret my soup-pouring behavior.

So, for example, instead of merely noting that someone chews gum when he enters a classroom and then predicting, "He has a poor attitude about my course," it is more prudent to try to find at least several of the indicators that are predictive of the attitude in which you are interested. If you know which performances you will accept as your meaning of an attitude or other goal, you will also know how to assess whether the attitude (tendency to perform one way rather than another) is in the condition you would like. You will also have clues about which performances to change in order to improve that condition; when someone changes what he *does*, others are likely to change the words they use to describe him. As an example, if a person has been labeled "hostile" because of his tendency to throw pies in the faces of his colleagues and then gives up this performance, others are likely to stop calling him hostile and begin referring to him as reformed, or mellowed, or as having had a change of heart.

Notice that nothing in this discussion has had anything to do with behaviorism . . . or any other sort of ism. The concern with what people do and what they say does not stem from any sort of philosophical base. We are concerned with behavior because we have no other choice, no other route into the heart or mind of a person. It is the only sound basis we have for judgments about what is happening inside another human being. No matter how deeply we may desire that someone "internalize his growing awareness" or "feel a deep appreciation for the value of trees," the only evidence we have of the existence of such conditions is the person's behavior — what he says and what he does.

To make a goal more achievable, it is useful to know the meaning of the goal in terms of the performances that would cause you to agree the goal has been achieved. This is the purpose of the goal analysis, *one* tool to use toward derivation of meaningful outcomes of instruction. Since knowing *when* to use a tool is a significant part of knowing *how* to use it, we will begin with some practice in recognizing situations in which it will pay you to rummage through your toolbox for the goal analysis.

PART ⬜⬜
When To Do It

3

Recognizing Fuzzies

A manager had just reviewed a task analysis of an important position in his firm. "Yes," he said, "these are the skills we want the man to perform; but we also want him to *communicate a positive attitude toward the company.*"

Now when we are talking about a skill, whether of the mind or of the hand, we can easily determine whether it exists in the shape we would like. In the case of a manual skill, we simply ask to see it. Where a mental skill is concerned, we ask the person to perform the skill and then indicate the result of that performance with an overt (visible or audible) behavior (as when we ask someone to write down the answer to an addition he has performed somewhere inside him). But what about attitudes? What does a person do to "communicate a positive attitude toward the company"? Say nice things about the company? Whistle while he works? We don't know. It could be any or all of these things, or hundreds of other things. Until we know what the person who wants to achieve this state *means* by the statement, we cannot decide how to achieve the state; we cannot know when we are successful. We cannot decide *whether* to teach or *what* to teach.

That is when the goal analysis is used. Whenever one of these abstractions (or *fuzzies*) shows up as something important enough to do something about, *then* is the time to use goal analysis. The goal analysis will unfuzzify the abstraction to the point where you can say whether there *is* any useful meaning and, if so, what the essence of that meaning might be.

Intents to develop such states as "favorable attitudes," "deep appreciation," or "sense of pride" are examples of abstractions; they do not tell us what a person would be doing when he was demonstrating the state or condition, nor do they suggest the behavior that would indicate how we can tell he has done it. On the other hand, items such as "writing," "decanting," and "hopping" are examples of performances; they *do* tell us what a person would be doing when demonstrating his ability to do it. (Can you tell when someone is writing, decanting, or hopping? Yes. Therefore, you are dealing with performances.)

To check whether we are thinking along the same lines, examine the intents listed below. Some are fuzzies (abstractions) and some are specifics (performances). *Check the fuzzies*; then read on to see how well we agree.

1. __ name ten examples
2. __ appreciate music
3. __ feel a sense of pride in his developing comprehension
4. __ recite a poem
5. __ select a specimen
6. __ develop a sense of comradeship in attaining common goals
7. __ develop awareness of children's potential
8. __ have a religious dedication to one's profession
9. __ defend liberties
10. __ write a report
11. __ be a good citizen
12. __ identify fuzzies

Compare your responses with the comments on the pages that follow.

1. __ name ten
    examples

Can you tell what someone is doing when naming examples? Of course. He is either saying something or writing something. Naming is a performance.

2. ✓ appreciate music

What is someone doing when appreciating? Sighing? Breathing hard? Reciting the history of music? Playing a piece? The expression doesn't indicate or even imply the performances that constitute the meaning of the abstraction. This is a fuzzy.

3. ✓ feel a sense of
    pride in his
    developing
    comprehension

Mmm . . . important, maybe. But definitely not a performance. Ask the key question: What would someone need to do to convince you he had achieved this goal? *Those* are the performances; this is a fuzzy.

4. __ recite a poem

A performance. We would all agree on what someone is doing when reciting.

5. __ select specimens

This is a performance, but a somewhat subtler one. A few comments regarding this intent follow the final item.

6. ✓ develop a sense
    of comradeship in
    attaining common
    goals

Ah, a beautiful sentiment, and perhaps a worthwhile goal to attain; but definitely a goal (fuzzy) and not a performance.

7. ✓ develop awareness of children's potential

More of the same. If the target population is meant to be children rather than teachers, this item would be a double fuzzy; it would be talking about those doing the instructing instead of those intended as the targets of the instruction. A goal.

8. ✓ have a religious dedication to one's profession

This one is such an abstract abstraction I would even hesitate to give it the label of goal (it's more like a mission). It is of about the same caliber as "get the country moving again." The words have a lovely ring to them, but they don't provide the basis for making decisions about how we would know one if we saw one. "Having a dedication" isn't at all at the same level of specificity as "having a baby."

9. ✓ defend liberties

Again we have a nice-sounding goal. We can easily nod in agreement about its importance, but we would be hard put to say what to do to increase liberty-defending skills or recognize a liberty-defender when we saw one. It doesn't matter that what a person might do to defend liberties is different in different situations; until we know what those things are, we can't make improvements.

10. __ write a report   We may disagree about the cri-
                               teria by which a given report
                               should be judged, but there is
                               not likely to be any disagreement
                               (unless you are the troublemaker
                               type) about what someone is do-
                               ing when he is writing a report.
                               Writing is a performance that
                               is directly visible (and often
                               audible, if you find writing as
                               hard as I do).

11. ✓ be a good citizen   This might be number one on
                               the hit parade of fuzzies. It's cer-
                               tainly important, but what's he
                               doing when he is being a good
                               citizen? What would you take as
                               evidence that Sturmun Drang
                               qualifies for the good citizen
                               award? Would it be different if
                               he were a first grader than if he
                               were a senior citizen?

12. __ identify fuzzies   This one is similar to the "select
                               specimens" intent, and I'd like
                               to comment on it at some length;
                               but it will be easier to explain if
                               I can write all the way across the
                               page instead of in this scrunched-
                               up space.

The point is that some performances are visible and some
are not; and, since many of the best things we do are done
inside us, we don't want to eliminate internal (covert) performances from consideration. Hopping on one foot, for

example, is something you can see directly. The same is true of writing a report, singing a song, and welding a joint. *Adding*, on the other hand, is something you can *not* see someone doing.

Now don't interrupt!

Isn't it possible that you could add some numbers together even though you were tightly bound hand and foot and dangling from the highest yardarm? And isn't it possible that in that same trussed position you could *identify* the culprits responsible for the trussing, assuming they were visible? I'm not suggesting you should spend your time hanging around adding, only that it is possible to add without doing anything visible (overt).

You may be able to tell *when* someone is adding by watching his lips or his pencil, but you are not watching the adding. The visible behaviors you see, such as lip-moving and pencil-squiggling, are behaviors *associated* with the adding or are the *consequence* of the adding; but they are not the adding. A written or spoken number (correct or incorrect answer) may be the *result* of the adding, but is not the adding itself. So, even though adding isn't directly visible, we'll call it a performance, because it is possible to make a *direct inference* about the shape of the adding skill.

The same holds for our two items, "select specimens" and "identify fuzzies." You can do all sorts of selecting and identifying and never let anyone know you had done anything at all. You do thousands of things "in your head" all day long. Sometimes you indicate the results of these activities by doing or saying something, and sometimes you don't. If you made a selection, however, or if you made an identification, I would be willing to refer to these activities as performances, since there is a direct way of telling the nature of what you did. You could point to the thing selected or grab the thing identified; underlining or circling would do just as well.

There is a simple test by which you can tell the difference between a performance and an abstraction. Find out whether there is a *direct* way to determine the nature of the alleged performance by asking this question:

Is there a *single* behavior or class of behaviors that will indicate the presence of the alleged performance, about which there would be general agreement?

If the answer to the question is yes, you have a performance. If it is no, you are dealing with a fuzzy.

Let's try the test on a few likely candidates. If you believe an item to be a performance, see if you can jot down an answer to the key question. I've filled in the first one.

	What single act, if any, might you ask someone to perform that will tell you whether the condition exists?	*Is this item a performance?*
1. adding numbers	say (or write) the correct answer	yes
2. identifying piranhas		
3. appreciating literature		
4. internalizing an appreciation		

I would consider only the first two items as performances. To find out if someone identified piranhas correctly, you could ask him to point to the piranhas. That is a single act that would tell you directly if the internal performance occurred. You could also ask him to paint a red dot on each piranha or put his finger on their heads. There are lots of *indicator behaviors* you could select from, so there *is* a direct way to sample the existence of the identifying. But what single thing would you have someone *do* to convince you he was appreciating or internalizing? Do you think everyone would agree with any indicator you might select? Unlikely. And what single act could you have someone perform to tell you he was internalizing an appreciation? (That's really an unfair question, for it is probably dealing with words without meaning. Such words may be popular parlance on the school scene, flung about with great abandon; but that doesn't guarantee they have meaning.)

One way to tell whether a statement is too broad to be considered a performance is to put the substance of the statement into the Hey Dad Test. You simply use the substance of the statement to finish this sentence: Hey Dad, let me show you how I can _____! If the result is absurd and makes you want to laugh, you are dealing with a statement broad enough to be considered an abstraction rather than a performance. For example: Hey Dad, let me show you how I can internalize my growing awareness! (Yeah? Lemme see you!)

Silly, isn't it? That's because we aren't talking about a performance, either visible or invisible. We are talking about an abstraction. Try another example: Hey Dad, let me show you how I can be satisfied with my goals! Not as funny, perhaps, but still rather odd. Now try this one: Hey Dad, let me show you how I can smile! Aha! Now that one has the ring of sense to it.

Try the Hey Dad Test yourself on the following items and see if it doesn't help you spot the performances from the abstractions:

ride a bicycle
add columns of numbers
be optimistic
be warmed by success
use the library as a source of pleasurable activity

If you would like a little more practice in recognizing the difference between performances and abstractions, go to the next page. Otherwise, go on to page 35.

Here are a few more items to help sharpen your ability to recognize performances and fuzzies. There are the usual three kinds of items on the list: performances, (1) some visible or audible (overt) and (2) some invisible (covert), and (3) abstractions (fuzzies). *Check the fuzzies.* Remember the key question: Is there a single thing a person might do to convince me he is demonstrating the condition described in the item?

1. __ smiles a lot
2. __ says favorable things about others
3. __ feels deeply about others
4. __ is confident in his ability
5. __ can recognize symptoms
6. __ is able to appreciate school
7. __ is able to manage with enthusiasm
8. __ knows how to compare prices
9. __ can discriminate business trends
10. __ able to assemble components skillfully

Compare responses on the pages that follow.

1. __ smiles a lot

A performance. You can tell when someone is smiling. We don't know what "a lot" means, but that is a question of the criterion of acceptable performance.

2. __ says favorable things about others

Can you tell if someone is saying things about others? Yes. So this item can be called a performance.

3. ✓ feels deeply about others

What is he doing when he's feeling deeply? We don't know, and can't tell from the statement. A fuzzy. Perhaps important, but a fuzzy nonetheless.

4. ✓ is confident in his ability

Same as the last one.

5. __ can recognize symptoms

Here is one of the covert performances. You may not be able to tell *whether* he is recognizing at any point in time (he can stand around perfectly still while doing his recognizing), but you can tell whether the results of his recognizing are satisfactory or unsatisfactory. You can tell directly by asking him to tell you something, point to something, label something, etc. The test is whether you can use a single indicator as evidence that the recognizing has occurred as desired.

6. ✓ is able to appreciate school

I'm sure *you* weren't fooled by the "is able to" opener, but there are still people who think that any sentence beginning with those words is automatically specific enough to be called an objective. That isn't the case at all, as this item illustrates. A fuzzy, not a performance.

7. ✓ is able to manage with enthusiasm

Same as the previous item.

8. ✓ knows how to compare prices

This is a little bit of everything. "Knowing," of course, is an abstraction; but "comparing" is something else. Can you tell if someone compared? You could ask him if he did and he might reply, "Yes, I compared." But that isn't any better than if he said, "Yes, I *know*." Actually, there are a number of things someone might be doing when comparing — noting those things that are the same, finding the smallest or the largest, etc. Can you name an indicator behavior by which we will know if his comparing is acceptable? If you are not sure, or if there is room for disagreement, better think of this item more as a mini-fuzzy that will have to be defined further.

9. ✓ can discriminate business trends

Similar to the last one. Again, because of the context, there is room for discussion about what "discriminate" means. Does this mean that he divines trends, that he points to trends when he sees them on charts, or that he senses them during the flow of a business day? By itself, we would have to consider it an abstraction that needs further clarification before we can agree on what he's doing when he's doing it. There are times, however, when "discriminate" is a performance. Consider, for example, "discriminate capital letters." Here you can find out directly if he can perform by asking him to point to the capitals, circle or underline them, poke a hole through them, etc. Any one of these indicator behaviors would tell us if the desired performance has taken place.

10. ___ able to assemble

Can you tell what a person is doing when he is assembling? Yes. He is putting things together. Again, we don't know what "skillfully" means, but that is a criterion of acceptable performance, a way of saying how well the person must do the performing.

SUMMARY SO FAR

A goal is a statement describing a broad or abstract intent, state, or condition.

A goal analysis is useful whenever a goal exists that is important to achieve, or to achieve better than is presently the case. It is used whenever a statement of intent describes an abstraction, when it doesn't answer the question, How will I know one when I see one?

A performance is an activity that is directly visible or audible (overt) or directly assessable. An invisible or internal (covert) activity can be considered a performance if it is directly assessable; that is, if there is a single behavior that will indicate the presence of the performance.

© 1971 United Feature Syndicate, Inc.

PART □□□
How To Do It

Getting It Down
(Steps One and Two)

Now it's time to plunge into the procedure itself, step by step. There are five steps, and each of them will be explained and illustrated with examples from life. A wide variety of examples will be used to help show how the procedure might be useful in your own world and to demonstrate that a lot of people in widely different circumstances have used the procedure to good advantage. After all of the steps have been explained and illustrated, a complete example will be offered — as it actually happened. And, finally, we'll consider some variations on the theme.

Step One of the goal analysis procedure is to write down the goal. Use whatever words are comfortable, regardless of how fuzzy or vague they may be. This is the place for such words. The reason it doesn't matter how broad the words are here is that this step is just to get you started and to help you remember what caused you to start analyzing in the first place. For example, your goal might be one of these six items:

> the student should have a good attitude toward school
> have pride in work
> develop a growing awareness of civic responsibility
> understand the needs of the environment
> create a successful marriage
> develop successful industrial relations

Note that the first item looks like a complete sentence and the other five are scraps of sentences. It doesn't matter. Describe the goal with any words that make you feel good. If you can make yourself feel good when you begin, you may be more likely to continue. (And you should feel good if you recognized "feel good" for the fuzzy that it is.)

There is another reason why it is useful to begin a goal analysis by writing down the goal. It is "politically" useful. We can almost always agree with each other on the importance of vaguely-stated intentions. So when people (or your boss) see your goal, they will know you are doing good things. To follow the thought a little further, just about *any* time you show someone your specific objectives, write the goal they define on the same page. It is often difficult for a layman to understand the significance of an objective; if he sees only the specifics, he is likely to grunt, "Why would anybody teach anybody *that*?" If he sees the goal on the top of the page, he is less likely to emit such disturbing sounds.

Check the goal to make sure it describes an *outcome* rather than a *process*, so that you don't get bogged down with the problem of means and ends at the very beginning. That is, make the statement say "have a favorable attitude toward carbuncles," rather than "learn to have a favorable attitude toward carbuncles." Make it read "understand _____," rather than "develop an understanding of _____."

To give you a little practice in making the goal talk about ends rather than means, here are a few practice items. Each is now stated in a way that will get the analyst in trouble, because each implies something about *how* the goal is achieved rather than what the goal state looks like when it *is* achieved. Fix each item by making it talk about ends (cross out the words that imply process).

1. Develop a fuller appreciation of the problems of the twentieth-century world.
2. The student grows to discover his appreciation for well-tuned clavichords.
3. Come to see that the pollution problem is important.
4. The student develops a sense of humor.
5. The student grows into an awareness of his natural surroundings.

Turn to the next page to see if we agree.

This is what the items on the previous page should look like.

1. Appreciate the problems of the twentieth-century world.

2. Appreciate well-tuned clavichords.

   or

   Have an appreciation for well-tuned clavichords.

3. Appreciate the problem of pollution.

   or

   Understand the importance of pollution.

4. Have a sense of humor.

5. Be aware of natural surroundings.

   or

   Have an awareness of natural surroundings.

Thus, the first step in the goal analysis procedure is to write down the goal and make sure it says something about the intended outcome rather than about the means for reaching it.

Step Two of the goal analysis procedure is to write down the things you would want someone to say or do to cause you to agree that he represents the goal. Use only words and phrases; make no attempt to tidy up the things you write down, and *don't* try to write objectives. Keep in mind that this is a scratch paper exercise.

There are four strategies that may help you complete this step of describing the meaning of the goal. Use whichever is most productive for you.

1. Answer the question, What will I take as evidence my goal has been achieved? What would cause you to be willing to stamp a person with the label of your goal? If you want a favorable attitude toward school, for example, what would it take to make you willing to agree that the attitude of

Jeremy Jimperly is in the shape you would like it to be? Jot
everything down that you can think of, without any thought
to duplication, without any concern for the fact that many
of the items are just as broad as the one you started with,
without any concern for the suspicion that some items may
not make the best of sense. If it will help, write on the very
top of your page:

First drafts are for getting **down**, not for getting **good**.

After all, you can't repair what you don't have. You can't
cross out things that aren't there. You can't rearrange invisible
items. Besides, thinking about what you would accept as
evidence of achievement of your goal is hard enough without complicating the matter by having to write down only the
things that make sense.

2. Answer the question, Given a room full of students,
what is the basis on which I would separate them into two
piles, those who had achieved my goal and those who had
not? After all, you *do* make judgments about whether your
students or trainees are acceptable in skill or attitude; you
do make statements about their understanding or motivation or feeling. Now is the time to lay on the table the basis
for those statements.

*Given a room full of students . . . how would you separate them into two
piles . . . those who had and those who had not achieved the goal?*

3. There is still another way to think about the performances that are the meaning of your goal. Imagine that someone else will be charged with the responsibility for deciding which of your students will be labeled with the goal and which will not be so labeled, and that you are going to tell him how to proceed. What instructions will you give him? What should he look for? *How will he know one when he sees one?* Suppose you want students who are conscientious. Never mind for the moment how they *get* that way or what you might do to achieve that state, think about the state itself and how you would tell someone how to recognize it. Should he look for people who:

> finish their work on time?
> ask for extra assignments?
> work neatly?
> stay until their work is completed?

Jot down all the clues you can think of. (Or, if you are the literate type, all the clues of which you can think.)

4. Think of someone who is one and write down why you think so. That is, think of someone who already has achieved your goal, someone who represents your goal, and write down the things he says and the things he does that cause you to be willing to pin that goal label on him. If, for example, your goal is to have students "appreciate music" or to have trainees "demonstrate pride in their work," think of someone who does appreciate music or who demonstrates pride in his work and write down the performances that cause you to say he has your kind of appreciation or pride. If you can *not* think of anyone who represents your goal, you have a problem. Perhaps your expectations are unreasonable. Perhaps the goal (as you perceive it) is unattainable. If so, then a change in expectation is in order.

If you cannot think of anyone who represents your goal, ask yourself this question: Is it reasonable or practical to expect to achieve this goal? If the answer is no, revise the goal to one that is reasonable and practical to achieve. If the answer is yes and you still can not think of someone who represents the state or condition described by the goal, you need to think of what a person *might* be like if he represented your goal. You are skating on thin ice, though, because when you think of hypothetical people, there is the danger that your expectations will be forever unattainable. It's much better to think of real people and to state why you are willing to point your finger in their direction and say they exemplify your goal. Suppose, for example, you want students "to be able to write effectively." Having written the goal, you would think of someone you know who writes effectively enough to suit you; then you would ask yourself why you are willing to say so. What does this person say or do that makes you willing to say he writes effectively? Could it be that he:

> uses good grammar?
> uses descriptive words?
> expresses ideas in the fewest possible words?
> gets the results he wants?
> causes the reader to respond as he desires?
> gets the reader to repeat his ideas with relative accuracy?

Whatever you think might be the basis for your judgment, write it down.

You can approach this step from the *positive* by writing down the performances you *do* want to see to convince you your goal is achieved, and this is the approach to take whenever you can. When you find yourself unable to make progress, however, you might approach from the *negative* by writing down performances that you *don't* want to see, performances that would represent non-examples of what someone would have to do to convince you he represents your goal. Examples of each of these approaches follow.

EXAMPLES FROM THE POSITIVE

Safety Consciousness. This example comes from a group of industry managers whose company had an accident record higher than they thought reasonable. The showing of safety films and the display of safety posters didn't seem to have much effect. The managers decided they wanted to be more successful in achieving safety consciousness in their employees, so they decided to take a closer look at this goal. Following the procedure described in Step One, they wrote the goal on a flipchart: "safety consciousness."

The next step was to remind each other of the things they would take as evidence of safety consciousness, to tell each other the things that safety-conscious people say and do.

"Well," said one manager, "I think of old Joe Carson as being safety conscious, because he reports safety hazards whenever he sees them."

"Yes," said another, "and he wears his safety equipment."

A third then added, "A safety-conscious person is one who follows safety rules, whether they are posted or not. That is, he adheres to what is generally considered safe practice."

And so it went. Each item mentioned was written on the flipchart as a potential part of what these men *meant* by safety consciousness. After half an hour or so, their list looked something like this.

safety consciousness

reports safety hazards
wears safety equipment
follows safety rules (no infractions)
practices good housekeeping (keeps his work area free
    of dirt, grease, and tools)
encourages safe practice in others (reminds others to
    wear safety equipment)
says favorable things about safe practice
suggests ways to improve safety record

This, then, was the main basis for deciding whether a person was safety conscious or not. These were the performances that would cause one of the managers to pin the label of "safety consciousness" on someone. This was therefore the essence of their *meaning* of the goal of safety consciousness.

Pride in Work. Here is an example of a more difficult goal, one that proved harder to define. The faculty of a dental school decided that a very important goal for their graduates to achieve was "pride in work." They explained, somewhat facetiously, that they didn't want their graduates leaning over their patients muttering things like, ". . . y'know . . . I never *really* wanted to be a dentist in the first place." Though not meant to be taken seriously, the comment did suggest something about what this faculty meant by *lack* of pride.

After writing down the goal "have pride in work," these gentlemen were urged to think of the things a dentist might say or do to make them willing to pin this label on him. In this case, as in many others, it wasn't easy to get started. After all, though we often talk to each other in the broad terms of goal language, we seldom think very seriously about just exactly what we mean by those nice words.

After being reminded that (a) we were just trying to put down *possibilities* from which to select and (b) there was no need for agreement about what was put down, one of the men offered an opening shot: "Well, at least *I* would never say anybody had pride in his work if he didn't do his assigned work on time." (If this sounds a little defensive, it is probably because people aren't used to being challenged to expose the basis for their judgment, especially on such affective matters as "pride in work." So, if you are ever in a position to help people define their goals, write down *whatever* is said quickly and, in the old brainstorming manner, refrain from passing judgment on what is said. That comes later.)

Once the ice was broken, a half hour of discussion produced the following jottings:

have pride in work

carries out assigned tasks on time
finishes tasks regardless of the time required
carries out his tasks regardless of whether others carry
    out theirs
finishes, or reports, unfinished tasks left by others
carries out tasks completely, leaving no loose ends
performs most tasks at the level of his ability
speaks favorably about his profession
speaks favorably about well-performed tasks
dresses in a manner befitting his profession

You can see that for this group the essence of "pride in work" had mainly to do with how tasks are carried out. *You* may mean something completely different, and others may have still other meanings (if that were *not* the case, there would be no need to clarify goals). But this faculty has done everyone the courtesy of making *their* meaning visible. *Now* they are in a position to discuss their meaning, to wonder whether it is the best meaning for their situation, to work at improving the meaning, and to write the objectives that embody the essence of the meaning. And once they've done that, they can act to achieve their goal more effectively than ever before.

Love of Learning. More and more teachers are concerned these days that their students have a favorable attitude toward learning. They are interested in doing those things that will enhance a love of learning rather than detract from it. They understand that the old-fashioned "if it don't hurt, it ain't learning" approach was more likely to drive students away than attract them to greater interest in knowledge, and they want to apply what is known about the

principles of human performance toward better achievement of the "love of learning" goal. Before they can do that,
however, they must know just how they would recognize a
learning-lover when they see one.

One such group of teachers set about the task of increasing the number of their students who, in their estimation,
were favorably disposed toward learning. They began by
trying to say how they would know one when they saw one.
Their initial list looked like this.

<u>love of learning</u>

works willingly at school projects
seeks additional opportunities to learn
reads widely (more widely than school subjects)
asks questions when he doesn't understand
comes to school ready to work (with paper and pencils)
works at his best level
is a self-starter
has initiative

Notice that the list trailed off into some fuzzies, as do
most lists the first time around. The sorting procedure that
followed took care of that. At this stage, the main thing was
to get everything down that might help them to know one
when they saw one.

EXAMPLE FROM THE NEGATIVE

Sometimes it isn't easy to get started scratch-papering the
performances by which you would recognize achievement of
your goal; sometimes it isn't easy to start describing how to
recognize one when you see one. Oh, well. If you can't get
in the front door, try the back. If you can't get started with
the positive, try the negative. You can *always* think of several
performances that are clearly *excluded* from your meaning
of a goal. You can always think of things a person might do

that would cause you to say, "*That* sort of performance is certainly *not* representative of a person who _____," or "*He* certainly doesn't deserve to be called _____," or "Well, I know one when I see one, and *he* isn't one!" Once you have started listing some of the performances you *don't* want to see, you can usually turn them into the positive performances you *do* want to see.

Good Personality.   Let me illustrate how this works with an example developed with some hotel managers who wanted their bartenders to have "good personality." If any goal ever qualified as a fuzzy, this is it. Suppose someone handed you a clump of students and said, "Here. Go teach these people to have good personality." What would you teach them? Where would you begin? How would you know if you had succeeded?

You may not much care about the personality of bartenders, but those who employ them and those who use their services do. (Bars used to be just places to gather for a bit of hail-fellow and good cheer; now they seem to be more like group therapy centers.)

The attempt to think of the performances that would cause them to agree a bartender had a good personality left the managers nothing but blank paper. They couldn't for the life of them get started in listing the things that would cause them to point their finger at someone and proclaim "good personality."

So, we tried from the other end.

"Have you ever fired a bartender?" they were asked.

"Have we ever!" was the reply.

"Tell us about them," was the request.

And they did. Within minutes, a half-dozen characteristics of the *un*acceptable bartender were listed by the hotel managers.

The acceptable bartender is *not:*

sour
humorless
abrupt
blameful of customer
aggressive
of gloomy appearance (unsmiling, unwashed, scowling)

Could you help but notice that all the items on this list are fuzzies? You will often find this to be the case. But first drafts are for getting down, not for getting good. Don't worry about what the first try looks like, because there is a way to handle the problem. Simply put each fuzzy on a separate sheet of paper and start over; repeat the process until you reach the performances that are the essence of your meaning. The hotel managers did that with their negative fuzzies, and they turned them positive as they went. Before long, they had statements like these:

1. Handles glasses with care, without spilling or slamming.
2. Smiles visibly when serving or addressing customers.

And as soon as they had these statements written down, they said, "But wait a minute. Those things don't have anything to do with good personality!" And maybe they were right.

But who cares? Vague terms are interchangeable, and "good personality' was just a place to start. There are any number of other goals they might have started with that would have served as well, such as "friendly person," "empathic with customers," or even "be a good Joe." The key issue is whether the two statements they came up with represent important performances.

The managers then said, "But wait a minute. *Those* performances are trivial!" — the same charge that is made about a great number of instructional objectives. The reply to this charge is that the test of triviality is not in the words of an objective or in a statement of performance. You cannot tell whether the item is trivial merely by reading it. *The test of triviality is in the consequence of not achieving the performance.* If there is no consequence when the performance is absent, one might well entertain the thought of triviality. But if there is a consequence, then the performance is not trivial, no matter what words are used to describe it. In the case of the present example, the conversation went something like this.

"What happens to a bartender who spills stuff on customers?"

"We *fire* him."

"What happens if a bartender doesn't smile regularly?"

"We fire him, too."

What is trivial about being fired? That is really something in the way of a consequence. Since it *matters* whether they are careful and smiley, these performances are not trivial, regardless of how the bartender might feel inside; therefore, the objectives that will ultimately describe these intended outcomes will not be trivial either. It doesn't matter whether the words in the objective are long ones or short ones, the test of triviality is not in the words but in the consequence.

SUMMARY SO FAR

The first two steps in the goal analysis procedure are these:

1. Write down the goal, using whatever words best describe the intent.
2. Write down the performances that would cause you to agree the goal has been achieved, without regard for duplication or fuzzinaciousness.

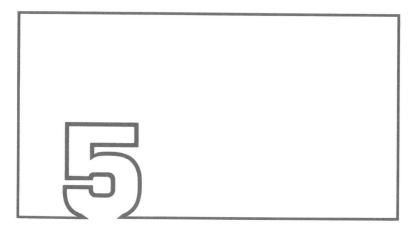

Sorting It Out
(Step Three)

Once you've jotted down the things you think might cause you to agree your goal has been achieved, you will need to go back over your list and do some tidying up and sorting out. Why? Because if your list is anything like the ones I've seen or developed myself, there will be all sorts of cats and dogs on it. For one thing, you are almost certain to find items that are at least as broad or abstract as the one you started with. Those who begin to say what they mean by "initiative," for example, often write down "is responsible." Similarly, those who begin to say what they mean by "is responsible," write down "take the initiative." This is not difficult to understand. In conversation we use lots of words that either say the same thing or nothing at all. Lots of vague terms are interchangeable, you see, so there are bound to be a number of fuzzies making their way onto our list. We want our students to be conscientious, we say. Oh, and what does that mean? Why, it means we want them to be responsible.

And what does responsible mean? Well, it means we want them to have pride in their work. And *that* means we want them to be dedicated. And around and around we go, defining one fuzzy with another. Little wonder we don't experience as much success with the so-called affective domain as we'd like.

On your list you may also find redundancies or duplications, things you have said in more than one way. In addition, you may find some items that, on second thought, can be crossed out simply because they don't say what you want to say.

You may occasionally find some items that describe procedures rather than outcomes, means rather than ends. These are to be deleted, for the object of the analysis is to figure out how to know one when you see one, not how to make one.

Finally, you may find goals that are administrative rather than instructional — goals that can only be achieved by an institution, not by an individual student. For example, an item such as "reduce absenteeism" is not something a student or trainee can do anything about. It is an administrative goal. You may wish to change the item to "have no unexcused absences," because that is a characteristic of an individual. But, unless you are defining institutional goals, items that have to do with groups are not for your list.

Step Three of the goal analysis procedure is to sort the things you have listed in Step Two:

1. Look over the list and cross out duplications and items that, on second thought, you don't want.
2. Check the abstractions (fuzzies), so you will know which items you will have to put on separate pages for further analysis.

Here's an example of how it goes. While working toward analysis of a goal described as "demonstrates initiative," a group of managers listed these items during their first time around.

enjoys responsibility
makes good decisions
uses good judgment
is on time

After completing the list, they went through the items for sorting. The first item is a double fuzzy. Both words describe general states. Both are inferred from the things you might see someone do or say. Since the managers agreed that this was an important item for further consideration, they labeled it a goal and went to the next item.

They thought about the second and third items. Although good judgment was an important quality, they felt that what they were really interested in was good decision-making. Since good decision-making was the main thing they meant by good judgment, they threw out the latter item as being essentially a duplication of the former.

Finally, they thought about the last item. "Yes," they said, "we can tell directly if someone is on time. He's either there at the appointed hour or he isn't. All we have to do is say what we mean by 'on time,' so that a criterion of acceptable performance will be available." That was easier said than done, however, for there was quite a discussion about just what the limits of "on-timeness" should be. But that was real progress, since they were now discussing the desired shape of a performance rather than arguing about abstractions.

Reworking their list, they now had:

√enjoys responsibility
√makes good decisions
is on time

The first two items, having been checked as goals, were put on separate pieces of paper; a new analysis was begun for each. The third item, already qualifying as a performance, was shelved until the performances defining the first two goals were identified. Once that was done, the managers were ready for the final steps in the goal analysis procedure.

Another example showing how sorting is done is this one involving a group of teachers concerned with achieving the goal "have a positive attitude toward school." Part of their list looked like this.

    no fighting on the playground
    no talking back to the teacher
    parents demonstrate a positive attitude toward school
    likes to come to school
    is ready to work
    reduce student vandalism
    decrease in classroom disturbance
    reduce instances of filthy language
    happy countenances
    teach children respect for property

Why not try your own hand at sorting this list out before reading how the teachers handled it? Check the fuzzies, draw a circle around each performance, and put some other mark by the items that look like administrative goals or instructional procedures (these will have to be turned into instructional goals or performances or be deleted). Then read on to see what actually happened.

The goal the teachers were interested in was for students to "have a positive attitude toward school." The sorting discussion went something like this.

"What about the first item, 'no fighting on the playground'?"

"That sounds more like a school rule than a performance, but we can turn it into a performance. How about 'doesn't fight'?"

"That's OK. We can count the number of times a student gets into a fight, if that is important to us. Let's label that one a performance."

"What about the second item (no talking back to the teacher)?"

The discussion on this item revealed that it wasn't what they really had in mind. They recognized there are times when the student should be encouraged to express disagreement with the teacher's views. What is more, they felt they couldn't achieve another of their goals (independent thinker) if students were never allowed to express their views.

"What we are really thinking of is insolence, disrespect, or insults to the teacher. These might also be indicators of 'attitude toward school,' so let's call insolence and disrespect goals to be further defined; and, along with them, we'll list 'doesn't insult the teacher' as one of the performances."

The next item, about parents demonstrating a positive attitude toward school, was quickly seen to be inappropriate. They saw that although it might help a student's attitude if the parents' attitude were positive, it is silly to define one person's attitude in terms of somebody else's attitude. This item was deleted.

"What about the likes-to-come-to-school item?" was the next question.

"Well," someone replied, "this one looks like the one we started with. What's the difference between a student's liking to come to school and having a favorable attitude toward school?" Since no one could think of a useful difference, the item was deleted.

"Is ready for work" was tackled next.

"That's a performance," someone said.

"No, it isn't," was the reply.

"Yes, it is," was the response. "I can tell when students are ready for work."

"How do you tell?" she was asked.

"By whether they have pencil and paper with them," she offered.

"No kidding. I tell by whether they have their homework ready to hand in," said another.

"And I," said a fourth, "tell by questioning them on the reading assignment."

A few minutes later, it was clear that each person felt he could easily say what he meant by "is ready for work" and that there were several performances (bringing pencils, bringing homework, etc.) that might be used as the meaning of the item. It also became clear to most that "He is ready for work" is a *conclusion* or inference made on the basis of the various performances described. The item was finally deleted, however, because it was "covered" by another of their goals.

"Reduce student vandalism" caused a small problem. The teachers were so concerned about the vandalism in their school, and so intent on getting action to reduce it, that it took several minutes and some discussion before they were able to see that, important though it may have been, the item as written was an administrative goal. It was a goal for school administrators to try to achieve, not for students. No single student can achieve a goal that talks about the performance of a group.

"But you can tell whether a student is vandalizing or not," someone said.

"Yeah," snided another, "if you can catch him at it."

It isn't difficult to say which performance constitutes vandalizing, but the teachers reworded the item and added it to their list of fuzzies anyhow. It doesn't need *much* defining, they noted; but, since "vandalizing" is an abstraction that could be defined in terms of a large number of performances, further thought was indicated.

"Decrease in classroom disturbance" and "reduce instances of filthy language" are both stated as administrative
goals; but, since they implied performances that were important to the teachers, they were reworded to read "does
not disturb class" and "does not use filthy language." Then
they were added to the list of goals about which the question
would be asked, What do we mean by "disturb" and "filthy"?

When the teachers got to the second from the last item on
the list, they had a good laugh — and merrily deleted it. Surely
they wanted happy countenances on their students' faces,
but it was pretty clear to them that they were not going to go
around counting smiles as part of what they mean by favorable
attitude toward school (though smile-counting is not an
unreasonable thought).

"Well, what about the last item (teach children respect for
property)?" someone asked. Here again, there was some
discussion before it was clear that this sounded more like
an instructional procedure, a *means* by which the original
goal might be achieved. Since they felt they had pretty well
covered the matter with their vandalism item, they deleted
this one.

What they had left was this:

~~doesn't fight~~
✓ is not insolent/disrespectful (i.e., no insults to teacher)
✓ doesn't vandalize
✓ does not disturb class
✓ does not use filthy language

— four goals and one performance.

"And all *negative*," said one teacher when he looked at the
list. "These are all *non*-behaviors. Don't we mean anything
positive by 'favorable attitude toward school'?"

The sentiments this teacher expressed were the result of
an event that occurs regularly during the goal analysis pro-

cedure. People discover that their view of what they mean by a goal, especially an affective one, is essentially negative. They discover that they have been thinking largely in terms of "don'ts" rather than in terms of "do's." A group of principals working on an analysis of "likes school" drafted a first list that consisted solely of discipline items, all twenty-three items. Items such as these abounded: "doesn't litter," "doesn't write on walls," and "doesn't make trouble." Once the principals saw these items written down, they were appalled; they began to ask whether these items represented what they "should" mean by the goal.

But what you "should" mean by your goal, what performances are the best indicators of a goal achievement, are questions to answer *after* you have put your "now" meaning on the table. To answer these questions may take a literature search as well as a soul search; at least some information is available about the behaviors that are reasonable meanings of various abstractions. Our current concern is with how to describe what you *do* mean when you utter a goal statement; how to *improve* that meaning involves procedures other than goal analysis, procedures that are, unfortunately, beyond the scope of this book.

Since you will encounter the "nonbehavioral definitions" during one analysis or another, I thought it best to prepare you for the shock of discovering that there are times when you expect to determine whether someone has achieved a particular goal by noting the *absence* of behavior. No need to be concerned, now that you are forewarned. After all, there is nothing necessarily wrong with defining a goal in terms of the *absence* of behaviors (how many of the Ten Commandments call for non-behavior?) if that is what you intend to mean. But is usually *isn't* what you mean, which suggests the need for some more scratch paper thinking. In the "favorable attitude toward school" example, the teachers would have had to label *every student* as one who had achieved the goal if there were no detected instances of fighting, insolence, vandalism, class disturbance, or filthy language; and they were not willing to do that. They felt that there simply *must* be more to their meaning of that goal, and so they decided to meet again to look for some positives.

SUMMARY SO FAR

The goal analysis procedure so far, then, is this:

1. Write down the goal.
2. Jot down the performances that, if observed, would cause you to agree the goal has been achieved.
3. Once a goal has been written and a list has been drafted of the things you think would cause you to agree the goal has been achieved, the list is sorted out. Duplications are deleted, as are the items that, on second thought, are unwanted. Abstractions are checked and performances are marked in some other, handy-dandy fashion. Each goal (abstraction) is then written on a separate piece of paper. The process is repeated until every item remaining is either a performance or a nonperformance, either a "does it" or a "doesn't do it."

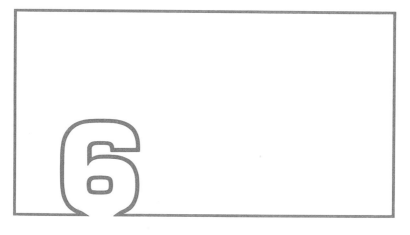

Putting It Together
(Steps Four and Five)

Step Four of the goal analysis procedure is that of making coherent statements to describe what you intend for each of the performances on your list. These statements describe the outcomes you must achieve to be willing to say your goal is achieved. This step will facilitate your testing of the performances to see if they truly reflect what you mean by the goal, and it will assist you in deciding what to do to achieve the goal better. For example, in analyzing a goal of "likes music," an instructor listed these performances:

plays an instrument regularly
identifies music he likes

Now it is one thing to know what the performances that represent the essence of your goal are, but it may be something else to know the nature or amount of those performances that would cause you to agree the goal is achieved. The instructor in this example had to ask himself not only

what he would consider as "regularly," but also what he
meant by "identify." When he did so, he had these statements drafted:

> The student takes lessons on a musical instrument of his
> choice, or plays the instrument of his choice at least three
> hours each week.

> Without references, the student is able to write the titles
> and composers of all music for which he expresses a pref-
> erence (liking).

The instructor agreed that, for practical purposes, he would
be willing to say a student liked music if these conditions
were met; but he was uneasy about the criteria he had im-
posed. "Where do I get off saying that a student doesn't
like music if he plays less than three hours each week?" he
asked. That is a good question; but only *he* can answer it,
since the purpose of the analysis is to help him say what *he*
means by the fuzzy. If, upon reviewing his meaning, he decides it needs modification, the analysis will have served
its purpose.

If you think the instructor's statements are foolish things
to mean by "likes music," write down your own meaning
and make a comparison. If you still think the performances
aren't what someone ought to mean by "likes music," it
might help to remind you that we are not terribly concerned with whether the performances that define a goal
are really, really *the* meaning of the goal. Since so many
terms are interchangeable, it doesn't appear too useful to
hunt madly for *the* meaning any more than it is useful to try
to define the "good teacher." The search for *the* meaning
is rather like the search for the handle on a fog. Much more
important is the search for the substance of the goal, those
individual performances that you want to see happen or not
happen, regardless of whether they represent *the* meaning.

The task before us at this point is to write a description of each desired performance, usually in the form of a complete sentence. *These sentences can then be tested collectively for their adequacy or completeness, the fifth and final step of the goal analysis procedure.* Here are four examples to show how it works.

A Case of Consciousness. The goal was for production employees to be "more security conscious," because the plant manufactured classified military products. During the second step of the analysis, the managers doing the work quickly discovered that their main concern was with the way in which sensitive documents, such as blueprints, were handled. When they were finished, they had written:

security conscious

does not leave classified documents unattended
locks up materials

Though these statements describe things you might see a person doing or not doing, they do not answer the question, What will you take as evidence the goal has been achieved? They do not yet suggest how to know one when you see one, how to tell when someone does or does not qualify for the goal label. The managers who completed this analysis quickly understood the problem; they asked each other what would be a reasonable expectation with regard to the desired performances. Before long, the following statements were drafted (thus completing the fourth step of the analysis):

A person is said to be security conscious when:
1. There are no instances in which he has been found to leave sensitive documents unattended.
2. His filing cabinet is always found locked when he is not on the premises (i.e., leaves for the day or leaves the room in which the cabinet is located).

How will they know one when they see one? They will know one when they find a person who has never left sensitive documents unattended and whose files are always locked during his absences. That person will be called "security conscious." Anyone for whom they have counted one or more instances of unattended documents or open files will not be considered "security conscious."

They were then ready for Step Five, the last step in the goal analysis procedure, testing the statements for adequacy. To do this, one asks: If someone performed according to the statements, would you be willing to say he represents the goal? That is, if a person did all the things the statements call for him to do, would you be willing to say he has achieved the goal to your satisfaction? If the answer is no, you must decide what *else* you want from him for you to consider him satisfactory. You must decide what is missing from your meaning of the goal. If the answer is yes, your analysis is complete. (When I say your analysis is complete, I mean that you will have identified what you currently mean by the goal in terms of people performance. I do not mean to imply either that your meaning is the best possible meaning or that you should not try to bump your meaning up against reality so that it will be consistent with what is known and with what is practical.)

In the present example, the managers asked themselves if they would be willing to say a person was "security conscious" if he locked his files and didn't leave classified documents unattended. Their answer was, "Well, yes; but only insofar as the care of documents is concerned." Therefore, they were finished with that part of their analysis. If, on the other hand, their answer had been no, they would have had to find out what was missing in their meaning of the goal. They would have had to find the missing essence of their meaning of the goal.

Now that the managers had a clear idea of what they were looking for, they were in a position to do two things they couldn't do before: (1) determine the current extent of security consciousness (i.e., count the number who were security conscious according to their own definition) and (2) decide what actions to take to increase that number. And *that* is precisely what the analysis is for.

A Case of Gas.   This example was developed by a high school instructor who wanted his students to "understand gas welding." As you might guess, this teacher worked in a vocational area, and he wanted his students to be able to have a comprehensive knowledge (there's a nice fuzzy for you) of the subject. His initial list of items had several fuzzies on it, such as "know how gas is produced," "understand metals," and "appreciate flame adjustment." Sorting led him to identify the performances that he was not concerned about. When he drafted statements about each, his meaning of "understanding" turned out to be:

The student who understands gas welding is able to:

1. Explain production of oxygen and acetylene gases.
2. Explain methods and precautions to be observed while handling oxygen and acetylene cylinders and equipment.
3. Assemble gas welding components to the cylinders. Components will include regulators, hoses, blowpipes, and tips.
4. Select proper tip and oxygen-acetylene pressures for workpieces of the following type (list added).
5. Adjust workpiece and blowpipe-tip handle for the flat welding position.
6. Light the torch and adjust to a neutral flame.
7. Establish and complete the weld while observing proper pattern and ending of the weld.
8. Shut down the welding unit and prepare it for storage.

Carrying out the final step, the test for adequacy, he asked himself *the* question: If someone did all these things, would I be willing to say that he understands gas welding? His answer was yes, so his analysis was finished. Now he was in a position (1) to determine the number of students who currently understand to his satisfaction and (2) to take steps to increase that number.

There are any number of things that one might mean by "understands gas welding," as you might guess. One might mean knowing the history of welding, knowing who is who in the welding business, and so on. Some people think that because the subject being taught is vocational, technical, or professional, it is therefore patently obvious what must be taught. This simply isn't true. In any subject area, there are a great many possible answers to the question, What is worth teaching? The answer may be somewhat easier to derive in subject areas that have meaningful outcomes to reach than it is in those that don't, but that shouldn't lead one to conclude that there are areas within which fuzzies aren't uttered. Have you ever heard a coach say he wanted his students to "appreciate physical fitness"? What did he mean?

A Case of Creativity.   Some of those who have, in my opinion, done the best job of defining their affective fuzzies are music educators. Not all, but some have taken great steps in identifying the essence of some goals generally though to be absolutely and indestructibly intangible. What follows is an example of what one group did with the goal "be musically creative." I can't tell you what their initial analysis looked like, since I wasn't present when it was completed; but I can show you the first draft of the sentences they wrote to describe their intended performances. Here is the essence of the skills they will expect of their students if they are to be considered musically creative:

musical creativity

1. Given the performance of a song by the instructor, improvise an accompaniment on a rhythm instrument.
2. Be able to improvise vocally a harmony part to a well-known song.
3. Be able to play by ear at the keyboard the melody of a given well-known song.
4. Given the performance of a song by the instructor, be able to improvise an accompaniment on a harmonic instrument other than the piano.
5. Given the performance of a song by the instructor, be able to improvise a harmony line on a melodic instrument.
6. Be able to create a melody and notate it. The melody should have a clear climax and a repose (feeling of resolution) at the end.
7. Improvise at the keyboard an accompaniment for a given well-known song.
8. Be able to compose or arrange music suitable for a brief (32 bars or more) dramatic presentation for performance by fellow students.

There it is. There isn't any question whatever about what a student will be doing when demonstrating his musical creativity. There are some questions to be answered about criteria, of course; but they can be answered when molding these statements into the form of acceptable instructional objectives. With the exception of the missing criteria, these statements are the answer to the question, How will I know one when I see one? They also provide strong clues about whether and what to teach.

A Case of Therapy. This final example is interesting because of the way the outcome descriptions compared with the goal. While working on the improvement of their curriculum, a nursing faculty decided that one of their goals is that students "be able to develop a therapeutic relationship with adolescents." This is a very "affective" goal, indeed. It was explained that it is extremely important for the nurse to be able to develop such a relationship with adolescents, as it contributes significantly to treatment success. Though an important goal, the faculty was not satisfied with their current success in achieving it. There were lectures on psychology and discussions about adolescents, but the number of students the faculty was willing to certify as having achieved the goal was too small to suit them.

Having written the goal, the next step, of course, was to list the performances that represented the goal. But this led to a heated discussion of several topics that appeared to be only peripheral to the main issue. There was talk of patients who were sloppy in their personal habits, and of nurses who left patients unnecessarily exposed while dressing or bathing them. There was discussion of several of the problems of being a nurse in this day and age, and of the things that happen in hospitals that make their lives dreary or cheery. But there didn't seem to be much discussion of what was meant by "therapeutic relationship." Finally, something happened. One of the women said, with an air of candor, "Look. Nurses aren't supposed to react to patients just because they're different." And within a short time, two statements that describe the essence of *their* meaning of "therapeutic relationship" were drafted. They were:

1. Be able to recognize patient characteristics to which the nurse should and should not respond (list of characteristics added).
2. Be able to respond with the proper skill, and withhold response, as indicated by patient characteristics (list of desired skills added).

In plain words, the first of these statements means that when a nurse sees a patient who is dirty or stinky, she isn't supposed to say "Yechhh!" If the patient is exceedingly homely or obese, or exhibits any other offensive or undesirable characteristics, the nurse isn't supposed to look or speak in a derogatory manner. Thus, the first statement describes an ability to recognize *when* to respond and when not to respond. The second statement means that when a nurse sees a patient to whom she is supposed to make a response, she has the skill with which to make that response. Note that the first statement is a pure visual-discrimination item that has nothing whatever to do with feeling (affective), and that the second statement describes some sort of cognitive-psychomotor (knowing-doing) skill that again has nothing "affective" about it.

Thus, the essence of a very affective-sounding goal had nothing whatever to do with feeling; nor do the statements describing the meaning of the goal have any affective words in them.

Nor should they. The basis for statements about abstractions such as "therapeutic relationship" is the things people say and the things people do. When we describe those things we want them to say or do to make us willing to label them with the abstraction, there is little need for fuzzies in those descriptions.

The procedure for clarifying goals has nothing whatever to do with humanistic or antihumanistic sentiments, or even with how "affective" the goal itself may be. To describe the world is not to change it. *To say what one means by a goal is neither to reduce the importance of the goal nor its profundity.* Though the meaning, when seen on paper, may appear trivial—or even *be* trivial—the act of writing it down means merely that what was once secret is now open for inspection and improvement.

SUMMARY

Once the performances representing the essence of the goal are identified, the final steps in the analysis are to draft statements describing each desired outcome and to test those statements with the question, If these performances are achieved, would I be willing to say the goal is achieved? When the answer is yes, the analysis is complete. The complete goal analysis procedure, then, is as follows:

Step One: Write down the goal.

Step Two: Jot down, in words and phrases, the performances that, if achieved, would cause you to agree the goal is achieved.

Step Three: Sort out the jottings. Delete duplications and unwanted items. Repeat Steps One and Two for any remaining abstractions (fuzzies) considered important.

Step Four: Write a complete statement for each performance, describing the nature, quality, or amount you will consider acceptable.

Step Five: Test the statements with the question, If someone achieved or demonstrated each of these performances, would I be willing to say he has achieved the goal? When you can answer yes, the analysis is finished.

7

A Complete Example

To some people, examples don't examp unless they are set within their own circumstances. This phenomenon, called the not-invented-here factor, or NIH, implies that unless a procedure was invented or developed for a particular area it couldn't possibly be useful to that area. But fuzzies are pretty much the same no matter where you find them, and I'm sure you can see that you can do the same thing about them here as well as there. The circumstances might be different, but the procedure is the same.

With that preamble, I am presenting a complete example of how the goal analysis procedure works in practice. The example happens to come from one particular industry; but when you see the first list of jottings, you will have to agree that it could just as well come from a setting similar to your own. To help show how the analysis progressed, each phase or major modification of the written work is presented as a *stage*. Please note that these stages do not coincide with the steps of the goal analysis procedure. The analysis took two days to complete.

STAGE 1

The problem was posed by a department in one of our telephone companies. Telephone operators, we were told, are not only expected to perform their tasks according to company practice and criteria, but they are also expected to perform these tasks with "good tone of service." Now the *tasks* to be performed were well described in a variety of manuals and documents, and there was fairly good agreement about how to tell whether the tasks are being performed properly. Not so with "good tone of service." Whereas you can watch the tasks being performed, you cannot see anyone "good toning." This is an "attitude," we were told; and, though experienced operators and supervisors show some agreement in their recognition of this attitude, there was less agreement about just what "good tone" is and how to teach it. "Good tone of service" was about as clearly understood as "enthusiasm" and "pride in work."

Twelve supervisors agreed to tackle the problem. After writing the goal, they worked in groups of two and jotted down words and phrases that would identify what an operator might do to deserve the label "good tone of service." The first round of discussion took about an hour, and the results looked like this.

Group 1	*Group 2*
courteous	pleasant voice expression
willing to help	well-modulated voice
receives positive response from customer	adequate vocabulary
	natural sound
makes grouchy customers happy	phraseology and judgment
	friendly, helpful manner
tries to make abrasive practices palatable	voice calm under stress
	informal — but businesslike
	patience

Group 3
enthusiastic
voice sparkles
rising inflection
interest
helpfulness
enunciates
rate of speech
vocabulary
phraseology
judgment
flexibility

Group 4
acknowledges pleasantly and
    appropriately and with ap-
    propriate answering phrase
sounds interested
inflection
keeps her cool
tries to calm irate customers
goes beyond call of duty
vocabulary
volume (not too loud – not
    too soft)
explains call delays in custom-
    er language
listens attentively

Group 5
doesn't sound mechanical
doesn't swear at customers
has empathy
recognizes customer may
    have a problem
answers promptly (within ten
    seconds)
expresses regret when ap-
    propriate (e.g.,
    customer is cut off,
    wrong number
    poor transmission)
doesn't interrupt customer
shows interest in customer as
    individual (e.g., tailors re-
    sponse to customer)

Group 6
speaks clearly
enunciates (not too fast – not
    too slow)
well modulated voice (not
    too loud – not too soft)
friendly and interested
good inflection (accents key
    words for meaning)
good choice of words
words understandable and
    palatable to customer (i.e.,
    customer reacts favorably)

Note that each group was trying to define precisely the same goal, that of "good tone of service." Though the lists were vastly different, there were a number of similarities; for example, some items appeared more than once. Note also the range of specificity of the items. Some were fuzzier fuzzies than the one we started with; others were quite specific.

If you are interested in a little practice, you might see if you can draw a circle around each item that describes an identifiable performance. Then go on to see what happened in Stage 2.

STAGE 2

Each list was written on a flipchart so that all could see what everyone else did in the way of goal definition. As you might expect, some lively discussion was stimulated when the wide range of meanings was exposed. Although some of the items were laughed at when put on the chart, the supervisors reminded each other that this was a first draft and, therefore, everything was acceptable. (It is important to allow time for casual conversation at this point, to help relieve whatever tension might be generated by the discovery that one's own meaning of something "everybody knows" may not only be not the same as everyone else's meaning, but may be different from *everyone* else's meaning.)

Once the conversation turned back to the analysis, the supervisors were ready for the next task, which was to identify which of the items were in need of further clarification and which described visible performance. This was accomplished in a little less than a half hour. It was decided to leave the fuzzies unmarked and to circle the performances.

The lists then looked like this.

Group 1

courteous
willing to help
receives positive responses
    from customer
makes grouchy customers
    happy
tries to make abrasive prac-
    tices palatable

Group 2

pleasant voice expression
well-modulated voice
adequate vocabulary
natural sound
phraseology and judgment
friendly, helpful manner
voice calm under stress
informal — but businesslike
patience

Group 3

enthusiastic
voice sparkles
rising inflection
interest
helpfulness
enunciates
rate of speech
vocabulary
phraseology
judgment
flexibility

Group 4

acknowledges pleasantly and
    appropriately and with ap-
    propriate answering phrase
sounds interested
inflection
keeps her cool
tries to calm irate customer
goes beyond call of duty
vocabulary
volume (not too loud — not
    too soft)
explains call delays in cus-
    tomer language
listens attentively

Group 5

doesn't sound mechanical
doesn't swear at customers
has empathy
recognizes customer may
   have a problem
answers promptly (within ten
   seconds)
expresses regret when ap-
   propriate (e.g.,
   customer is cut off,
   wrong number,
   poor transmission)
doesn't interrupt customer
shows interest in customer as
   individual (e.g., tailors response to customer)

Group 6

speaks clearly
enunciates (not too fast — not
   too slow)
well modulated voice (not
   too loud — not too soft)
friendly and interested
good inflection (accents key
   words for meaning)
good choice of words
words understandable and
   palatable to customer (i.e.,
   customer reacts favorably)

Only two of the six pairs of supervisors described anything in the way of performance. There could be any number of reasons for this; but once the group saw some actual examples of performance, they all saw the distinction between fuzzies and performances and moved ahead spiritedly.

STAGE 3

The next task involved some sorting. When there are several words that appear to have similar meanings, it helps to put them all into a group. When seen like this, those doing the analysis seem to have greater ability to eliminate items that are least descriptive of their goal. The items were rewritten on clean sheets of paper. Important-looking characteristics were written on the left, and words and phrases that appeared to define these characteristics were written on the right. The entire process took a little over an hour.

Characteristic	*Possible Meaning(s)*
enthusiasm interest beyond the call of duty sounds interested	voice sparkles (rising inflection) acknowledges pleasantly acknowledges with proper phrase
speech	rate enunciation — speaks clearly vocabulary phraseology
pleasant voice expression	volume (not too loud — not too soft) natural sound (doesn't sound mechanical) well modulated (doesn't sound mechanical) (variable pitch)
makes grouchy customers happy	tries to make abrasive practices palatable explains call delays in customer language voice calm under stress
courteous helpful manner patience willing to help keeps cool	doesn't swear at customer informal — but businesslike voice calm under stress words understandable and palatable answers promptly doesn't interrupt customer accents key words for meaning

empathy   ⎫   expresses regret when ap-
shows interest in customer ⎬   propriate (e.g., cut off,
    as individual   ⎭   wrong number, poor trans-
                                       mission)
                                   tailors response to individual
                                       (doesn't sound mechanical)
                                       (vocabulary)
                                       (phraseology)
                                   recognizes customer may
                                       have a problem

judgment

listens attentively

It doesn't matter very much whether these terms are "correctly" grouped, whatever that might mean. The grouping was only a way to help those doing the analyzing to think more clearly about what they mean by the goal.

Notice that "judgment" and "listens attentively" hang on the bottom of the list like little lost leprechauns. No matter. Items that stand alone draw attention to themselves.

STAGE 4

The next action taken was to narrow down the field by (1) eliminating those words and phrases that were redundant or didn't do what the analysts wanted and (2) defining those fuzzies that were considered important. The procedure followed was simply to point to each expression and ask whether it should be deleted or defined.

The result of the "sorting out" follows. One or two things were added during the process, and these additions are shown in brackets. Some items were crossed out because they appeared somewhere else, not because they were considered unimportant.

Characteristic	*Possible Meaning(s)*
enthusiasm interest beyond the call of duty sounds interested	~~voice sparkles (rising inflec-~~ ~~tion)~~ ~~acknowledges pleasantly~~ ~~acknowledges with proper~~ ~~phrase~~
~~speech~~	~~rate~~ ~~enunciation—speaks clearly~~ ~~vocabulary~~ ~~phraseology~~
pleasant voice expression	volume (not too loud—not too soft) natural sound (doesn't sound mechanical) well modulated (doesn't sound mechanical) (variable pitch)
makes grouchy customer happy	~~tries to make abrasive prac-~~ ~~tices palatable~~ explains call delays in cus- tomer language ~~voice calm under stress~~
courteous helpful manner ~~patience~~ willing to help ~~keeps cool~~	doesn't swear at customer informal—but businesslike ~~voice calm under stress~~ words understandable and palatable answers promptly doesn't interrupt customer accents key words for meaning

empathy
shows interest in customer
  as individual

                                expresses regret when ap-
                                  propriate (e.g., cut off,
                                  wrong number, poor
                                  transmission)
                        tailors response to individual
                                  (doesn't sound mechanical)
                                  (vocabulary)
                                  (phraseology)
                        recognizes customer may
                                  have a problem

judgment

listens attentively   [doesn't repeat questions]
                                  [records responses accurately]

The sorting-out process reduced the amount of vague verbiage to a point where the participants could begin to see what they would expect in the way of *performance* before they would be willing to label an operator as having "good tone of service."

STAGE 5

When the adding and deleting was finished, the supervisors could see that there were not only some things they wanted an operator to *do* as part of their meaning of "good tone of service," but that there were some things the operator would have to *refrain* from doing. (Though it is desirable to define an intent in terms of positives, or "do's," one should not hesitate to describe in terms of "don'ts" when there are intended constraints or restrictions. But these constraints or restrictions should always be an essential part of the goal's meaning.) So, it was decided to try to group the "do's" and "don't do's" into clumps. The result looked like this.

Actions	*Must avoid*
acknowledge requests	swearing at customer
express regret	interrupting customer
handle requests properly	banging*
discriminate between duty and	
beyond the call of duty	
listen attentively	
(criteria: accurate responses	
no question repeats)	

Action should be done with:

understandable words (vocabulary)
accenting of key words
proper phrase usage
variable pitch
calm voice (under stress and normal conditions)
responses tailored to the individual

STAGE 6

At this point, the supervisors felt they had finally identified the important performances and wanted to take a whack at describing their intents in the form of complete statements.

This was the result.

Good tone of service

1. Answers with proper phrases within two seconds of plug-in.

---

*"Banging" means to slam hands, books, or equipment in such a way that the customer detects operator irritation or frustration. If an operator feels she must vent her spleen by slamming her fist on her shelf, she is supposed to break the connection while she does so.

2. Handles customer requests (i.e., performs operator tasks):

<u>without</u>   <u>with</u>

swearing   words understandable to the customer
interrupting   key words accented
banging   using prescribed phrases
                              using variable pitch

3. Demonstrates an ability to listen attentively by responding to a series of typical calls (a) accurately and (b) without asking the customer to repeat the information he has given.
4. Given the following customer situations (list inserted), expresses regret by saying, "I'm sorry."
5. Given a series of taped or printed dialogues between operator and customer, is able to identify those calls in which the operator responded beyond the call of duty.

STAGE 7

The supervisors were asked if they would be willing to say that an operator had "good tone of service" if she did the things described in the five statements they had prepared. They tentatively said they would, but recognized with their discussion that there was still a little tidying up to be done. It would be easy to say what is meant by such things as "swearing," "proper phrase," "call of duty," and "typical calls," they said; but some of the phrases listed under Item 2 would need more thought. How would they tell if key words were accented? How would they decide if an operator's voice pitch was variable enough to suit them? To clarify one item, someone suggested that if the customer didn't have to ask an operator to *repeat* information, that would be a good indicator of "words understandable to the customer."

Someone then reminded the group that it was not up to them to pass final judgment on the company's meaning of "good tone of service." The analysis ended then when someone suggested the statements be drafted and forwarded for management review.

COMMENT

If you will glance back at the first list of "good tone of service" meanings and compare it to the final five statements, you will note quite a difference. The initial list consisted mainly of words reminiscent of the Boy Scout oath. If you will look at the various lists, you will see what is likely to happen when a person writes each first-list-fuzzy on a separate sheet and repeats the analysis for each. What happens is that the same performances begin to appear on list after list. Rather than finding this disturbing, I take it as a sign of progress, as a sign that I am finally finding what, to me, are the performances I care about most.

In the situation described in this example, what started as a broad but important goal ended up as five statements describing specifics. It is now possible for the trainers to increase the number of operators who have "good tone of service," and it is now possible for the supervisors to keep track of progress toward that end.

Do the five statements represent *all* there is to "good tone of service"? Probably not. Those who carried out this analysis will undoubtedly think of other desired performances. When they do, they will add them to their list of outcome statements and modify their training accordingly. *Until* they do, they have a basis upon which they can make sure each and every operator performs in accordance with the essence of the goal.

PART IV
Variations and Consequences

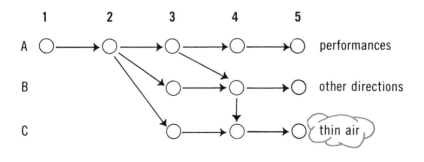

Surprise Endings

One thing you learn from repeated use of the goal analysis is that it doesn't always take you where you think you're going. Sometimes it does, as we have seen in previous examples, lead you to the performances that are the meaning of the goal, to the performances that need to be increased or decreased if the goal is to be achieved better. Sometimes, in other words, the analysis takes you through the five steps of the procedure as described (shown below as Track A).

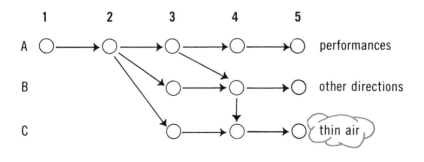

Sometimes, however, the analysis causes you to shift direction drastically; and sometimes it all evaporates into thin air. Instead of following Track A, as expected, you may find yourself following Track B or C. This shouldn't be particularly surprising, for it is a common phenomenon in everyone's life. You may go to the doctor with a firm idea of what you would like to have done, only to have his diagnosis show the problem to be something entirely different. You may go to the store to buy a new turn-signal light for your car, and later find that what you really needed was a fuse. Fixers of electronic devices sometimes find that their "trouble" disappears once someone remembers to plug the device in. So it goes.

And why not? Nobody's perfect; if we were, there would probably be no need for analysis procedures, especially the kind being described in this book. You start off in one direction, and analysis turns you in another. So? That's what analyses are for!

To help prepare you for the various outcomes you will encounter when analyzing your important goals, I'll describe some examples that show some of the other-than-as-planned things that can happen.

From Welfare to Embarrassment. The first example is from the nursing profession, where there is little question about the importance of their goals. While working to identify the specific skills important to the practicing nurse, the faculty noted that they wanted nurses to "show concern for patient welfare." When asked to describe the basis on which they would decide if someone did indeed "show concern for patient welfare," the discussion started easily and rolled along merrily. At the beginning, there was a great deal of talk about such things as empathy and sympathy, and the difference between these fuzzies. There was discussion about whether it was necessary for nurses to

"really like" their patients if they were to give effective
treatment, and about the problems of working with doctors
and aides. The discussion wasn't exactly pertinent to the
problem at hand, but one learns to allow for some rambling.
It seems to help people realize that they normally use quite
a few fuzzies during what they consider "technical discussions"; it helps them realize that they don't really know what
they are talking about when describing the goals they think
important. A little rambling helps clear the air. Asking someone to define his goal in terms of performances *he* would
accept is a little like asking someone to take his clothes off in
public—if he hasn't done it before, he may need time to get
used to the idea.

After ten or fifteen minutes had passed, someone finally
said, "Well, no one can be said to exhibit concern for patient
welfare if she leaves the patient unnecessarily exposed." And
the discussion took a sharp turn in a new direction. The
participants zeroed in on this topic immediately, and it became clear to those present that concern over "unnecessary
exposure" was of more immediate interest than "patient
welfare." No doubt items dealing with exposure would be
part of what they mean by "patient welfare" (vague terms are
interchangeable); but after writing the first item on their list
(which was a fuzzy), they zeroed in on it, tabling their initial
goal statement for later analysis. Within a minute or two, the
faculty had written:

Goal: Shows concern for patient welfare

1. does not leave patient unnecessarily exposed to:
   fear stimuli
   embarrassment
   treatment

And then, rather than continue defining *this* goal, there was
strong interest in abandoning it in favor of "unnecessary

exposure to embarrassment." Everyone came up with anec-
dotes (critical incidents) describing events leading to patient
embarrassment. In each case, the activity or condition leading to the embarrassment was jotted down; eventually, the
list looked like this.

Prevents patient embarrassment

1. controls number of visitors
2. does *not*: a. leave patient exposed physically
               b. treat patient in socially derogatory manner
               c. insult patient's values
               d. insult patient's medical knowledge
               e. bawl out staff in patient's presence
               f. ask more intimate questions than needed
                  to do the job

The remainder of the session was devoted to clarifying
the fuzzies on this list and to testing the list with "the question" to determine if it represented their meaning of "prevents patient embarrassment." So, what started out to be an
analysis of one goal, ended with the definition of another.

From Listening to Facilitating.   This is another
example of a change in direction in mid-analysis. A group of
English teachers said that an important goal in elementary
school was to teach kids how to "be better listeners." When
the goal was written on the chalkboard, there followed a
discussion of its importance. After a few minutes, the teachers
were reminded that the next step was to describe what someone might do who represented the goal. But for a time there
was only silence.

A lot of thinking . . . but silence.

Finally, one teacher ventured a cautious, "Well, we really
can't expect children to listen attentively if they don't have
good hearing."

Immediately, "good hearing" was written on the board.

That prompted another teacher to offer, "And we really can't expect them to listen attentively if it is *too noisy*."

"Not too noisy" was added to the list.

Then a third teacher said, "Yes, and we really can't expect them to listen attentively unless there is something *worth listening to*."

"Something worth listening to" was written down. Everyone looked at the board, and there was a long silence.

And then it seemed as though everyone started talking at once. This happened to be a sharp group of teachers, and they didn't need any prompting to see what had happened. They quickly saw that if they wanted more attention from the kids, they would have to make some changes in their *own* behavior and in the environment around the kids. A lively discussion followed about just what those changes would be and how they might be put into practice. So, what started out as an intent to write objectives describing what teachers would have to teach their children to make them better listeners, ended in a description of what the staff would have to do and what the environment would have to be to facilitate students doing what they already knew how to do.

From Appreciating to Nothing. An analysis that evaporated into thin air began with a group of instructors saying that one of their goals was for their students to come to "appreciate the problems of twentieth-century America." Here was a fuzzy of slippery proportions, as was soon discovered, for the items that began to appear on the scratch paper list described the problems themselves rather than ways to recognize someone who appreciated these problems. That point was quickly grasped; the instructors admitted that they didn't know how to recognize one when they saw one because they had never seen anyone who, in their opinion, would qualify for the goal label. They didn't know anyone who *is* one, but they wanted to create someone who would *be* one.

The discussion then lunged in another direction. The instructors agreed that twentieth-century problems were important and that their students should show some concern for them. They also agreed that the goal as stated was an unreasonable one to try to achieve. When they looked at their list of problems, they saw that each one they considered high in importance was either being attacked somewhere else in the curriculum or was of no concern to the curriculum (none of the school's business). Hence, problem solved. The goal was seen for what it was, a false start.

From Honors to Humility.   This example is interesting because of the path followed during the discussion. It comes from a session held by the members of a high school faculty who taught the advanced placement, or honors program, a program reserved for students ranked in the top one percent academically. The general purpose of the program was to give these brighter students an opportunity to *explore at greater depth* those subjects offered at the school. The faculty met because they were concerned about their program.

"Our goal is to improve the honors program," they said; and the discussion was begun. The goal was written on the chalkboard, and the teachers were asked what their students would look like if the program *were* improved. They were asked to imagine a student who had just completed the improved program and to describe the important characteristics of this student. The discussion moved slowly, with an air of hesitancy. Words were used cautiously, thrust into the air like the fists of a wary boxer sparring to gain knowledge of his opponent. Though the verbal sparring continued for twenty minutes, little progress was made toward describing an improved honors program.

"You know," one teacher suddenly said, "our problem is that other teachers accuse us of not having a different curriculum from theirs. They say we just make kids do the same thing but pile on more work."

"Is that true?" he was asked.

"No, it isn't," was the reply. "We *do* do different things, but we don't know how to prove it to the other teachers in the school."

As soon as this new definition of the "problem" was offered, every other teacher in the room voiced agreement. Other teachers were jealous of them, they felt. *They* wanted to be honors teachers, too. Since they weren't, they sniped; and that sniping was bothersome.

Here was the first change in direction. "Improve the honors program" was replaced on the board with "define the honors program." Now the discussion centered on how objectives might be written to describe honors program intents. It was felt that if these objectives could be made visible, everyone would see how the honors program differed from the regular school program. There were a number of comments about how the honors student was intended to be skilled as an independent learner and about how he was expected to be an analytical thinker. Again, little progress was made; it soon became clear that this was just another round of verbal terpsichore.

After a particularly noticeable hole in the discussion (silence, that is), one teacher ventured, almost aggressively, "What we *really* want to do is get rid of that darned arrogant attitude. Just because those honors students are in the top one percent of their class, they think they know it all. What we'd really like to do is send them away without that doggone cocky attitude."

And with that, the real problem was finally exposed. There it was, out in the open where all could see. It was quickly agreed that this indeed was the crux of the situation, that this was the important goal to be achieved.

This was the second major shift in direction. They had started with "improve the honors program," moved to "define the honors program," and settled on an intent to eliminate the cocky attitude. So, the eraser was wielded once again. The goal was changed from negative to positive, and written: "have a humble attitude when leaving the program."

Again, participants were asked to say how they would recognize a student with the intended attitude. Very quickly (within five minutes), the following items were written:

> he would test his knowledge
> his reactions to explanations by others would reflect:
> willingness to listen
> willingness to compromise
> willingness to consider alternatives
> willingness to consider another point of view
> eager to receive new knowledge no matter what the source
> collects and weighs information before coming to a conclusion or making a judgment

(When reading a first-draft list of "performances" written either by myself or by others, I am often tempted to say, "Hey! That's one of the finest descriptions of perfection I've ever seen." Such lists contain so many abstractions that they show how unreasonable our expectations often are.)

These items made it clear to the faculty that their main concern was with how the honors student behaved in discussions with others. The behavior of main concern was that of rejection of the contributions of others. The "arrogant attitude" was characterized by a general disdain for the comments of others, by a dogmatic conviction that their own position was correct because, after all, they were the brightest of the lot. A decision was made to concentrate on performance in discussions, and the fuzzies on the list were attacked in that light. The intent now was to decide how to count the number of their honors students who displayed the "humble attitude" during discussion of controversial topics when the discussion included students from outside their elite ranks. After some jocular remarks about how they were setting out to learn how to "count smartasses," and after the eraser had received a vigorous workout, the following items remained:

During discussion of controversial issues:

1. Allows others to finish presenting a point of view.
2. Acts to prevent others from interrupting presentation of a point of view.
3. Discusses others' points of view without insulting them.
4. Doesn't impugn the intelligence of others.
5. Supports his arguments or convictions with facts rather than with his intelligence (e.g., doesn't say things implying "It's true because I said it, and I'm smarter than you are").
6. Accepts (uses) information presented by others.

There was agreement that these were performances. The teachers felt they could recognize whether someone interrupted another speaker or tried to prevent an interruption. They could tell when a student was insulting another. They could tell when someone's intelligence was being "impugned," even though that word could stand some further clarification. They could, in other words, count instances in which each of these items occurred.

The next step was to test the items with "the question." If someone did these things, would they be willing to say he had a humble attitude? Well, yes, they would. They wanted to listen to some discussions to see if there were any important items left out; but, for the moment, they were content that they had defined the goal.

At about this time, one of the teachers asked, "How do you suppose these students develop an arrogant attitude?" and they were off again. Within minutes, these thoughts were offered:

> "They see a dogmatic teacher who behaves as though he must always be considered right. He doesn't leave any room for discussion. He makes it clear to students that their job is to come up with answers just like the teacher's answers."

> "The standards by which students are measured aren't appropriate. They are only compared with other students of the school, and always come out on top. They should be put on a different scale, such as comparing them with all the students of the city."

> "Students don't know where they stand with regard to experts on the subject. They know that they are better than others in the school, but they don't know how far they might have to go to be really expert."

And before they knew what had happened, they were off on a discussion of the actions they might take to develop the desired attitude. Now that they knew exactly what the desired student looked like, they were able to plan their own actions to help them achieve the goal more successfully. Among the possibilities discussed:

1. Teachers should be better models and act the way they want the students to act. They should be willing to explore questions with the students rather than demand pat answers. They should consider the students' points of view. They should let the students do more of the talking.

2. Teachers should show the students how true professionals (experts) act. They should bring in professionals
   so that students could talk to them, so that students
   would have a chance to compare their depth of knowledge to that of professionals rather than with that
   of their peers alone.

3. In addition to evaluating students on the basis of what
   they already know, and in addition to showing them
   where they stand in relation to other students in the
   school, show them how much or how little they have
   progressed during a given period of time. In other
   words, show students how much they have *advanced*
   in their *own* understanding rather than merely that
   they are farther along than others.

Quite a difference from where the discussion started (improve the honors program), or was it? I suppose one could
argue that the program would be improved when the faculty
took steps to decrease the "smartass count" and increase the
number sent away with an attitude of humility. But why argue
over a point like that? The goal you start with is just that, a
place to start. Let your analysis take you to your important
outcomes. If you discard the original goal along the way, or
modify it, consider that a sign of progress. Rejoice! The
teachers in this example started with a goal they thought
important and ended with the criteria by which they could
identify achievement of a goal of even greater importance.
And they knew what steps to take to do a better job of
achieving the goal. The goal analysis had served its purpose
well.

SUMMARY

Sometimes the goal analysis leads you to a definition of the
goal you started with, and sometimes it leads to the definition
of another. Sometimes you will be led to give up the analysis

in favor of a more urgent activity, and sometimes the content of the analysis will evaporate into thin air. So what? The purpose of an analysis is to give you better information with which to make decisions. If it does that, even by sending you in a different direction, you win!

9

Not for the Casual

This chapter is not for the casual reader or goal-achiever. It is for those to whom achievement of one goal or another is of the utmost importance or urgency.

This chapter is about attitude charting; more broadly, about goal or success charting. And why not? We've seen that it is possible to "tangibilitate" the meaning of an attitude by describing the performances we would accept as evidence that the attitude is in the shape we would like it to be. We've seen that if we know what performances to look for, we can count them when we see them. And if we can do that, why can't we plot the results on a graph? No reason at all. And if that goal of yours is as important to achieve as you say it is, then you will surely want to keep track of how you are doing. You will want to be able to compare the steps you take to the results they produce. You may not be able to plot with great precision, and probably wouldn't even want to; but, at the very least, you will want to make sure your actions are taking you in the desired direction.

There is nothing new about the value of indicator charting. Lots of people who care about their effectiveness do it. If you are a manager, you undoubtedly keep tallies and graphs showing progress in the events descriptive of company success. If you are a teacher, you probably keep track of test results and, perhaps, assignment completion and quality. If you are a physician or a nurse, you need no reminders about the importance of charting health (success) indicators. The only thing that may require a little getting used to is the fact that it is possible to plot the progress of indicators that define some very affective and intangible-sounding states. But it is possible, and it is being done.

For example, one school principal decided he wanted students to be "conscientious about school." A goal analysis told him that the main performances he was interested in were these:

> comes to school on time
> asks for additional assignments
> turns in assignments on time
> is prepared for work (i.e., brings paper, pencil, books)

He was perfectly well aware that others would define the goal differently. "But," he said, "I don't care whether these performances are what the faculty or I *ought* to mean by conscientiousness; these are the performances that would lead me to be willing to say that a student deserves that label." To increase the number of students who deserve the label, he would have to increase the number of students who exhibited these performances.

Once he knew what he was looking for, it was possible to prepare a simple graph to depict the progress of each item. He could plot the number of students who arrive on time, the number who ask for additional assignments, the number who turn their assignments in on time, and the number who arrive ready for work. His plots might look like this.

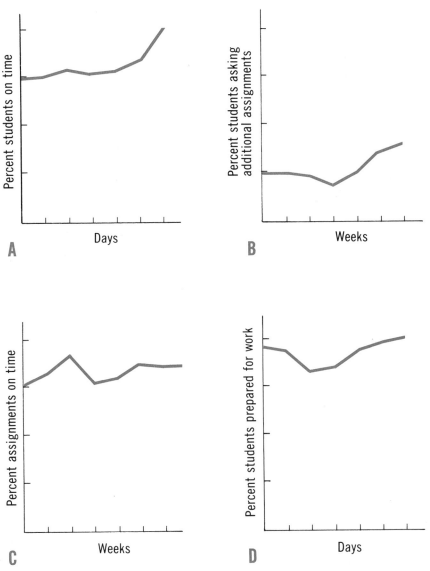

A

Percent students on time

Days

B

Percent students asking additional assignments

Weeks

C

Percent assignments on time

Weeks

D

Percent students prepared for work

Days

On the vertical line (ordinate), he would total the characteristic he is interested in. The horizontal line (abscissa) would show the frequency with which the count or assessment is made. The decision on frequency must be made on the basis of what is practical, of course; it would be nutty to try to plot something day by day, for example, when it is only possible to gather information month by month.

If things are going rather well for a characteristic, say attendance, one might plot deviations from the perfect. That is, instead of counting the number of students who arrive on time, it might be easier to note the number who are late.

Now then, if you are charting the performances that are the meaning of your attitude goal, aren't you plotting the attitude? Of course you aren't plotting the attitude directly, as there is no way to get a dipstick into wherever the attitude "is" for a direct reading—by definition. You can, however, plot the basis for your statements and judgments about attitudes; and that is just about as good. Better, in fact, since you can make adjustments as your meaning becomes more sophisticated simply by changing one or more of the charts. Does it matter whether you are *really* plotting an attitude? Isn't taking steps to see if you are moving in the desired direction the thing that matters? (Answer yes or yes.)

Perhaps you are thinking that the indications from each of the charts should be *combined* into a single indicator, and that *that* could be called the attitude chart, if anything is. Perhaps. It is certainly a tempting thought. But if you try it you are sure to be harassed, bludgeoned, and boiled in oil by the statisticians who understand such things. For one thing, it would be like adding apples and oranges, except worse. You can say that if you have three apples and four oranges you have seven fruits. But what have you got when you add three apples and four maps? Seven mapples? Seven something, surely; but it just isn't meaningful addition.

There is another problem with combining the content of the various charts, and that is that most of the charts are likely to have intervals of different sizes. That is, taking that first step toward perfection is a lot easier than taking the last step. If you were trying to lose weight, for instance, losing that first pound is generally a lot easier than losing the last pound. How much easier? We don't know for sure, and that's why it is not possible to combine charts. The size of the intervals isn't known.

You can combine if you want; but, since you won't know what the number will mean, you are running quite a risk. Fortunately, there is an alternative approach, one that doesn't require *anything at all* in the way of number-juggling skill. If you can draw a line, you're in.

What is *reasonable* to expect—in the way of attendance, for example? Is it reasonable to expect perfect attendance? Wouldn't you be willing to say that a student had a favorable attitude toward school even if he were absent once in a while, or late once in a while, or if he occasionally forgot to bring a pencil or a book?

In most cases, we are willing to accept something less than absolute perfection as our criterion of success. At least we do if we take into account the fact that people cannot often be expected to act with perfection, and the fact that our indicators may not be the best indicators of our goals.

And so enter the *zone of reason*. Rather than concern ourselves with combining graphs into a single indicator, let's make use of the zone of reason, that area on the graph you will accept as success. As long as the plot on the graph fluctuates within the area formed by the zone of reason, you can consider yourself successful. For example, consider the graphs presented on page 103. (As labeled, incidentally, they represent success achieved by the *school* rather than by an individual, because they describe performance exhibited by percentages of students.) Graph A totals the percentage of students who appear at school on time. Is it reasonable for a school to expect 100 percent promptness before it considers itself successful at influencing that kind of performance to occur? I don't think so. There are too many variables that might influence promptness that don't influence the way a person feels about school. If you agree, then what will you take? What *is* reasonable? Once you have decided what you will take as the mark of success, you can draw a line on the graph to represent it; then, whenever your line plots between that line and the 100 percent line, you can consider yourself successful in relation to that particular performance. For example, suppose you felt that 75 percent promptness is a reasonable expectation (we would be talking of a traditional, lecture-oriented school here, since promptness of arrival is a lesser virtue in an individualized school). A line would be drawn across the 75 percent mark, creating a zone of reason between 75 percent and 100 percent. As long as the promptness curve plots within that zone, you would consider yourself successful.

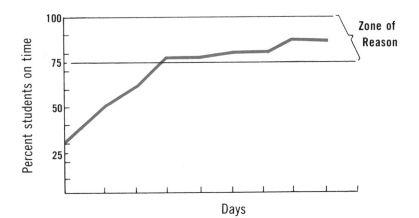

You might set your zone at different positions at different times. You might begin by noting what you get *now* in the way of the desired performance and then decide you will determine that your goal *for the year* is reached if you achieve a 5 percent increase. You would thus set your zone between 5 percent above current performance and 100 percent performance. Anything above 5 percent improvement is considered success and will cause you to agree your goal is achieved, at least so far as that performance is concerned.

In some instances, your zone may be formed not by two horizontal lines across the graph but by a triangle. As I sit at my typewriter squeezing out one sentence at a time, I look at a chart on the wall before me. This chart plots the number of pages that I type per day, and I have drawn a line that represents four pages per day as the minimum I tell myself I must do if I am to finish the first draft during the present century. As long as I do my four pages a day or better (even if I have to write letters to fill the quota), my plot lies within the zone of reason, the zone within which I tell myself I am "successful." (By thus defining success, I motivate myself

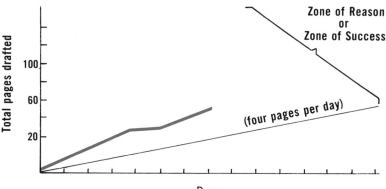

to keep at it by applying the theory of "divide and conquer." The thought of completing the entire project staggers me, you see; but, by slicing it up into little pieces and fixing things so that I can consider myself successful every day, I stick with it.) But that line will change as soon as the first draft is finished. A new chart will be prepared with a line representing more pages per day, for I expect to progress a little faster on a rewrite than on a first draft.

Where did I get the number four? From experience. It takes me two or three years to get my ideas developed and tried out to the point where I think there is something worth saying; but, when I sit down to say it, four pages per day on a first draft is all I can do. I suspect that *real* writers do a lot better than that, but a faster first-draft rate isn't reasonable for me. So *I* decide what I will consider to be the meaning of "success." If I do better than that, I will simply rejoice the more.

When managing an individualized course in which students are encouraged to move at their own rates, one finds that some rates are faster and some are slower (really?). But sometimes the slower student is slower because he is more thorough and more interested in the course rather than because he is less capable. After operating such a course a time or two, however, one quickly learns what the reasonable limits are. After all, one cannot allow a student to take forever to develop a set of skills, so there is a lower limit of tolerable rate. If a student progresses outside that lower limit, there is cause for corrective action. Occasionally, there is reason to set an upper limit as well; and if the student progresses faster than that upper rate, corrective action will also be taken. Many schools still demand that a student progress at a relatively fixed rate ("Don't try to get ahead of the class"), and in industry there are some managers with such confused notions about learning that they refuse to accept an employee unless he has been rooted in the real estate for a minimum time ("I don't care how smart this lad is; if he hasn't been in training for at least six months, I won't have him"). In cases such as these, the zone of reason will appear somewhere near the diagonal of a chart rather than above or below a horizontal line.

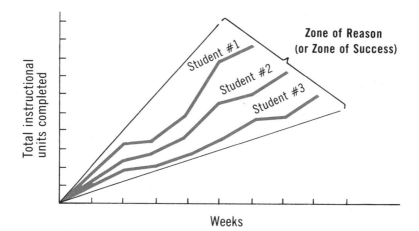

Suppose you set out to plot the performances that define your goal and find it difficult to collect the information you want. Suppose it turns out to be impractical to determine whether the performances you are interested in actually are occurring. Then what? Well, one of two things.

If you cannot collect the information you need to plot the performances, you have reason to wonder whether the performances are a reasonable meaning of your goal. If, for example, you define good citizenship in terms of what you expect a person to do ten years hence, you will find it impossible to find out if you are at all successful in achieving that goal. Sure you want your students to vote in every national election, but there is no practical way you can find out if they do. So, wonder if that is a reasonable meaning.

If you conclude that your definition is reasonable but that there is no easy way to collect information to plot . . . for now, that's OK. Nobody said that all fuzzies are easy to define (try a goal analysis of "reverence," for example). If you can't tell how you are progressing, you can't tell. Just make sure you refrain from labeling people as either representing or not representing your goal if you can't tell whether they are peforming as you want. If you know you can't observe the performances that are the meaning of your goal, just try to refrain from judging people in terms of that goal. For example, if part of what you mean by "loyalty" is "doesn't badmouth the company" and you can't tell the difference between badmouthing and constructive criticism, just hold off with the snap judgments about who is loyal and who is not. If you have no accurate way to find out what people are saying, or if you decide it would be unethical even to try, either change your meaning of the goal or refrain from making inferences about who is and who isn't one. But above all, try to remember that it is a highly questionable practice to label someone as having achieved or not achieved a goal state when you don't even know what you would take as evidence of achievement. That is almost as reprehensible as grading students on their "attitudes" when the basis for that grading is unknown and when the basis for the judgment shifts from one student to another.

A Choice of Conclusions

Before we bid fond adieu to the topic of goal analysis and sink slowly into the sunset, there is a matter that I would like to throw into your stream of consciousness. It isn't a matter of the utmost urgency, I admit; but it is important to those who have a concern for the techniques and details of what has come to be called instructional technology. It is a little matter occasionally bumped into by those workers who toil in fields where the expected crop is instruction that works.

I'll put it to you this way.

So far, you have examined a way to find the meaning of a goal that you consider of enough importance to warrant serious effort toward achievement. You have read through a variety of examples and have had a little practice with some of the steps in the goal analysis procedure. You have seen that the final step in the goal analysis procedure is to expand the descriptions of performance into statements that describe the way in which one would recognize whether the

111

performance was satisfactory, possibly by describing the main conditions under which the performance would be expected to occur and the extent of the expected performance.

Now if you know something about objectives, you know that to be worthy of the objectives label they must have pretty much the same characteristics as these expanded statements. They must describe a performance and the key conditions under which the performance is expected to occur, and they must provide an indication of the level or extent of the performance that will be considered acceptable.

That much is straightforward. No problem.

But now let me ask *you* a question. Is there such a thing as an *affective* objective?

Those who work to describe their important outcomes in the form of objectives have been told — by "them" — that behavior is of three sorts: cognitive, psychomotor, and affective. (You may even have had these terms flung in your direction on one occasion or another.) One implication in the use of these terms is that if there are three different kinds of behavior, there must also be three different kinds of objectives. Whether this is the case or not, quite a number of folks have been writing statements that they have been calling "affective objectives," mainly, I suppose, because they feel that they are being specific about the abstract states they hope to achieve with their objectives. They realize that many of their important intentions have to do with what are generally referred to as attitudes and appreciations. Not wanting to be guilty of ignoring these matters, they write a statement saying something about these intentions; having done that, they then refer to these statements as "affective objectives."

On the other hand, there are those who say, "Well, you can write objectives about cognitive things, but you can't write objectives about affective things" or "You can't write

objectives about attitudes, because attitudes are intangible."
The sentiment being expressed seems to be that if something is intangible, then it can't be concrete; or, perhaps, that
one shouldn't try to be specific about abstractions, because
such actions would somehow change or destroy the abstraction.

But we have been dealing with attitudes and other fuzzies
all the way along. We've gone from the fairly fuzzy to the
frightfully fuzzy and, in each case, described one or more
performances around which objectives could be written. For
a wide variety of abstractions, we've seen that a good part,
if not all, of their meaning can be described.

So, again, is there such a thing as an affective objective?

Yes . . . . **turn to page 114.**

No . . . . **turn to page 115.**

Depends on what you mean . . **turn to page 116.**

Yes? Well, you certainly have a point. Once a goal is analyzed for its meaning, it is possible to write objectives that describe the outcomes to be sought if the goal is to be said to be achieved. In this sense, it would be possible to call these objectives "affective," since they are the objectives that collectively define the goal. Then, when anyone asked you whether you had prepared objectives to describe your affective intents, you could legitimately answer in the affirmative.

Since it is likely that *every* objective could be considered as part of the meaning of one affective goal or another, you could even argue that *all objectives are affective objectives.*

Turn to page 117.

No? Well, you certainly have a point. By the time you have written a bona fide objective, you won't find any "affective" words in it. By the time you can define the performances that are the meaning of the goal, the fuzzies don't filter down (or up) into the statements of objectives. And when you look at any of the goal-defining objectives *separately*, you won't find any affective words in them as the action term. How could you?

Since to be called an objective it must describe a performance, and since performances are either cognitive or psychomotor, you could argue persuasively that there is *no such thing as an affective objective.*

Turn to page 117.

Depends on what you mean? Ah, you *are* the sly one! Imagine being skewed on my own barb. Trying to get me to say what I mean, are you? You've got a lotta nerve. Don't you realize what a catastrophe there would be if we all went around saying what we mean? What would happen to the politicians, the poets, and to those who go around internalizing their growing awarenesses? I'd suggest you ask people what they mean with a great deal of caution; clarity isn't exactly a popular commodity.

Anyhow, now that I can't evade your answer any longer, I'd have to agree that you certainly have a point.

If an objective is a statement that describes a performance that partly defines a goal, then you would want to say that *all* objectives are affective objectives, since every one can be considered part of what is meant by some affective fuzzy or another.

If, on the other hand, an objective is a statement that describes a performance, something you want someone to be able to *do*, then *no* objectives are affective objectives, since there are no affective action words in the statement by the time you have described a performance. You would then say that there are lots of affective goals, but no affective objectives. If it isn't measurable, it isn't an objective. If it is measurable, it isn't abstract. Since affective goals are abstract by definition, there are no affective objectives.

Turn to page 117.

So, the answer to the question, Is there such a thing as an affective objective? is yes, no, and depends. Everybody can claim to be right! What a happy situation! Whatever our position on this questionable issue, we can all rejoice in our rightness.

Actually, there is one class of objectives that *might* warrant being referred to as affective. These are the statements describing an intent to change an approach or avoidance tendency in a student or group of students where the indicator behaviors are spelled out. These would be statements such as:

Increase by 10 percent the number of approach behaviors toward school by the end of the year (list of behaviors included).

Decrease by 35 percent the number of avoidance behaviors exhibited toward the library by December 1 (list of avoidance indicators added).

At the end of my influence over the student, the percentage of approach responses to my subject (list attached) will be at least as great as it was when the student first arrived.

These statements describe an intent to increase or decrease the incidence of behaviors used as indicators of increasing or decreasing attitude toward a subject or activity. Since the list of indicator behaviors is appended, the statement of intent is measurable; since the behaviors are intended to indicate collectively the presence of an affective state, perhaps the statement describing that intent can be referred to as an affective objective. This is not to imply that there is no difference between the cognitive and the affective, or that there are probably an infinite number of visible behaviors that might be used as indicators of an affective state. It isn't even to deny that affective tendencies can be demonstrated in the absence of any cognitive knowledge at all. The point is simply that if a statement of intent describes the behaviors by which achievement of the intent will be indicated, that achievement is measurable and the statement can be called an objective. I suppose you could call it affective if you wanted to, since the situation is similar to when an objective includes a description of the fuzzy it is defining, such as:

The Goal

Demonstrate an understanding of _____
by being able to _____.

The Objective

Before getting all tangled up in the "does she or doesn't she" question, ask yourself *this* question:

Does it matter?

Is the question important? Does it matter how we label our objectives as long as they are stated in a way that they can be achieved?

What matters more is whether a goal is mistaken for an objective. Fuzzies that are labeled as objectives give their writer a false sense of security; he thinks he has said what he means when he hasn't. Most, if not all, of the statements currently called "affective objectives" aren't objectives at all, affective or otherwise. They are fuzzies. Here are a few examples pulled almost at random from a small mountain of such.

- Demonstrate your ability to perceive components and relationships in character motivation and action.

- Show your understanding of similarities and differences among sounds.

- Show your understanding of military obligations.
- To reveal to students the impact of one of the first types of literature to startle people to an awareness of the evil within themselves.
- Demonstrate a measure of personal growth, thereby achieving a higher level of maturity.
- Given a speaking-listening situation, the student demonstrates that one of his primary concerns is with the ideas that are being communicated.
- The student recognizes that most people give a great deal more time to speaking and listening than to reading and writing.

Each of these statements is alleged by its writer to be an "affective objective," but even the most casual examination reveals they aren't objectives of any sort. What is the performance mentioned in the statement? There isn't any. The writers have fooled themselves into thinking they have written an objective when they haven't, and have thus fooled themselves into thinking they have described their affective intents with enough clarity to know one when they see one.

So, although the difference between goals and objectives has practical implications on how well we succeed at achieving our intents, does it matter whether the objectives be labeled "affective" or not? I confess that I don't know. *What is important is to say what we mean well enough to know one when we see one, so that we can make better decisions about getting there,* and to be sure to include those affective intents we believe important to achieve. That's what the goal analysis procedure is for.

PART V

A Summary of Sorts

Let's Pretend

Rather than finish things off with a dreary summary that might send you away with your attitude all wrinkled up, it might be more useful to check out your ability to comment on the topics presented in this book.

Let's pretend you are talking with someone who knows you have just finished reading this book. This person is mildly curious, but doesn't know the territory. He/she is the Fuzzy-minded type whose vague feeling is that only intangibles have "real" value, and that anything specific or measurable is automatically base or trivial. He/she seems to believe that those things that are obscure or impossible to understand are somehow profound, and that those things that are clear or simple cannot possibly be worthy of his/her respect.

I'll provide his/her side of the interview, and you provide the replies. Afterward, you can compare your sharp and pungent explanations with mine and check your replies with the relevant text.

Heshe: Goal analysis, huh? What's that? Do you know
           enough about it to describe it in a sentence or two?
You:

Heshe: Why in the world would you want to do a goal
           analysis?
You:

Heshe: But how would I know *when* to do a goal analysis?

You:

Heshe: How would I know one of these broad statements
           when I saw one?

You:

Heshe: Can you briefly describe the steps in doing a goal analysis?

You:

Heshe: What will I be able to do when the analysis is finished?

You:

Heshe: Well, maybe *your* subject is trivial enough to be reduced to a bunch of little performances, but *mine* is intangible.

You: *(Watch your language.)*

Heshe: Oh, yeah? Well, let me tell you something. My goals can't be chopped up into little pieces. Besides, you don't think its necessary to analyze *every* goal to its last ounce of meaning, do you?

You: (*Steady now.*)

Heshe: HMMMmmmmmmmmmmmm.

If you'd like to compare your responses with the sort of thing I might say, turn to the next page. You might also want to check your accuracy by reviewing the text.

Heshe: Goal analysis, huh? What's that? Do you know enough about it to describe it in a sentence or two?

Me: Sure, goal analysis is a procedure for helping to define broad goals to the point where their main elements (performances) are described. It is a way to discover the essence of what a goal means.

Heshe: Why in the world would you want to do a goal analysis?

Me: Some goals are quite important to achieve. The goal analysis will help, because it will help you describe what you mean by success, help you know one when you see one. If you know what it is you want to achieve, and know what that achievement looks like when you have it, you can make better decisions about how to get there.

Heshe: But how would I know *when* to do a goal analysis?

Me: Whenever you have a broad statement of intent that is important to do something about.

Heshe: How would I know one of these broad statements when I saw one?

Me: Easy. A broad statement describes an abstraction, such as "understand," "develop," "know," "internalize," or "appreciate." If the statement doesn't answer for itself the question, How would you recognize one when you saw one? it's a goal.

Heshe: Can you briefly describe the steps in doing a goal analysis?

Me: Yes.

First, write down the goal. (Step One)

Second, jot down the performances that define the goal. (Step Two) Do that by answering whichever of these questions seems more relevant or comfortable to you.

  a. What would a person be doing that would cause me to say he has achieved the goal?
  b. Given a room full of students, what is the basis on which I would separate them into two piles, those who had achieved the goal and those who had not?
  c. How would I recognize goal achievement when I saw it?
  d. Thinking of someone who *does* represent the goal, what does he do or say that makes me willing say so?

Third, go back over the list and tidy it up. (Step Three) Cross out duplications and items that, on second thought, are not what you want to say. Carry out Steps One and Two for any remaining fuzzies.

Fourth, describe each important performance in a statement that identifies the manner or extent (or both) of the performance you require to be satisfied the goal is achieved to your liking. (Step Four)

Finally, modify these statements until you can answer yes to this question: If someone achieved according to these statements, would I be willing to say he has achieved the goal? (Step Five) Collectively, these statements are the meaning of the goal.

Heshe: What will I be able to do when the analysis is finished?

Me: You can do a number of things. You can take steps to find out how things are now going in regard to the performances you want, you can take steps to get more or less of each of the desired performances separately, and you can chart your progress.

Heshe: Well, maybe *your* subject is trivial enough to be reduced to a bunch of little performances, but *mine* is intangible.

Me: Perhaps you're right. And if so, it means there is no way to tell whether you are achieving your goals; therefore, you mustn't claim you are doing so. Unless you perform a goal analysis on your intangibles, you will never know which of them can be achieved better, nor by what means.

Heshe: Oh, yeah? Well, let me tell you something. My goals can't be chopped up into little pieces. Besides, you don't think it's necessary to analyze *every* goal to its last ounce of meaning, do you?

Me: No. Only those goals that are important to achieve, or to achieve better. *You don't change the world by describing it, but you put yourself in a better position to move things in your direction if you know what that direction is. So, goal analysis is not for every goal. Only for those that are important.*

Heshe: HMMMmmmmmmmmmmmm.

Selected References

KAPFER, M. B. "Behavioral Objectives in Music Education," *Educational Technology,* Vol. XI, No. 8, August, 1971, pp. 30-33.

MAGER, R. F. *Developing Attitude Toward Learning.* Belmont, Calif.: Fearon Publishers, 1968.

MAGER, R. F., AND PIPE, P. *Analyzing Performance Problems.* Belmont, Calif.: Fearon Publishers, 1970.

THIAGARAJAN, S. "Programmed Instruction in the Affective Domain," *NSPI Journal,* Vol. X, No. 6, July, 1971, pp. 5-10.

Book Fixers Exposed !

PRESS RELEASE   For release upon receipt

At a hastily—called press conference attended by
two editors and a clerk—typist, Robert Mager,
maker of miniMagermanuscripts, ripped the lid
off the secrecy surrounding the development of
his current work, Goal Analysis. Not only did he
name names, he identified just who was associated
with each phase of manuscript testing. Those
present gasped at the revelations.

When asked whether their contributions weren't
extremely useful in improving the manuscript,
Mager grudgingly replied, "Oh, sure. If it wasn't
for them the whole thing would be a shambles. They
made me throw out exampless examples and not—so—
funny funnies; they choked on things that turned
them off, and gagged at explanations that didn't
explain. Instead of finding a wall to write on,
they scribbled all over my pages with suggestions
for improvement and ideas for alternatives. But
it all came down to the same thing. Work, work,
work!"

"Do you think there is something to be gained
from exposing these kindly souls to public glare?"
he was asked.

"You bet I do," he replied energetically. "Once
they are known, they'll get what's coming to
them."

Mager then passed out sheets listing the testing
phases used during manuscript development and
the names of those assisting with each phase.
They are printed below for the amazement and
admiration of the reading public, and for raucous
cheering by all.

1. Continuity check (does it all hang
   together?): Dave Cram, John Warriner.
2. Content check (does it do what it is supposed
   to do?): Margo Hicks, Ed Krenz, Sue Markle,
   Sarah Morris, Maryjane Rees, Andy Stevens,
   Phil Tiemann.
3. Attitude check (does it contain unnecessary
   turnoffs?): Dorothy Carver, Jim Hessler,
   Bill Hicks, Dan Kratocvil, Frank Moakley,
   Vernon Rees, Charles Selden, Nancy Selden,
   Walt Thorne, Jack Vaughn, George Whiting.
4. Word check (are there obscure words that can
   be traded in for common ones?): Brad Mager,
   Randy Mager.
5. Cover check (are title and cover designs
   responded to favorably?): Vince Campbell,
   Jerry Harrison, Jeanne Mager, Debbie Michaels,
   Sarah Morris, Richard Neidrich, Laura Newmark,
   Peter Pipe, Oscar Roberts, Bud Robertson,
   Bill Shanner, Jim Shearer.